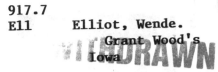
DATE DUE

GRANT WOOD'S
IOWA
A Visitor's Guide

Wende Elliott and
William Balthazar Rose

THE COUNTRYMAN PRESS
WOODSTOCK, VERMONT

PREVIOUS PAGE: **Woman with Plants** (*1929*), *Grant Wood*
Oil on upsom board, 20½ x 17⅞ in., Museum purchase. 31.1.
Cedar Rapids Museum of Art

Maps by Paul Woodward, © The Countryman Press
Book design and composition by Eugenie S. Delaney

Library of Congress Cataloging-in-Publication Data are available.
Grant Wood's Iowa 978-0-88150-992-2

Published by The Countryman Press, P.O. Box 748, Woodstock, VT 05091
Distributed by W. W. Norton & Company, Inc., 500 Fifth Avenue,
New York, NY 10110
Printed in the United States of America

10 9 8 7 6 5 4 3 2 1

I dedicate this book to my children, Sam, Henry and Eleanor,
who make all road trips around Iowa a raucous adventure.
—**Wende Elliott**

I dedicate this book to my wife,
Wende Susan Elliott, who encouraged me to return
to the United States after a 10-year absence and
brought me to the state of Iowa for the first time.
—**William Balthazar Rose**

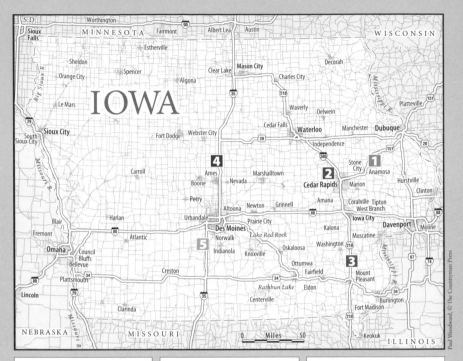

1 Anamosa & Stone City

Antioch One-Room Schoolhouse

Grant Wood Gallery and Visitor Center

Anamosa State Penitentiary

Riverside Cemetery

Stone City Art Colony

Grant Wood Art Festival

4 Ames

Parks Library

Morrill Hall, Christian Petersen Art Museum

Iowa State University Campus Art Walk

Memorial Union, Fountain, and Veterans Memorial

Ames Post Office Murals

2 Cedar Rapids

Cedar Rapids Museum of Art

Grant Wood Studio & Home

Turner Mortuary

Veterans Memorial Building Stained-Glass Window

J. G. Cherry Plant

Cedar Rapids Schools

Coe College, Stewart Memorial Library

5 Des Moines

Herbert Hoover Birthplace

Prairie Buffalo Sanctuary

Governor's Mansion

Iowa State Capitol

Des Moines Art Center

John and Mary Pappajohn Sculpture Park

Joslyn Art Museum

3 Southeast Iowa

Grant Wood's House

Plum Grove Historic Home

U of I Campus, Art Museum, and Art Department, Iowa City

Figge Art Museum, Davenport

American Gothic House, Eldon

Amish Community, Kalona

Amana Colonies, Amana

Tipton Carnegie Public Library, Tipton

Dubuque Museum of Art

CONTENTS

Van Antwerp Place (*1922–23*), *Grant Wood*
Oil on composition board, 12⅞ x 14⅞ Gift of Harriet Y. and John
B. Turner II. 72.12.78. Courtesy of Cedar Rapids Museum of Art

FOREWORD

I f Iowa had an official state artist as it has a state bird and a state tree, that artist would surely be Grant Wood, whose artistic output is indelibly linked with the landscape and people of Iowa. In fact, the image on the reverse of the Iowa quarter is a detail of Wood's painting *Arbor Day* and the image chosen for the stamp commemorating Iowa's sesquicentennial was a detail of Wood's painting *Young Corn*.

Even though Wood died in 1942, the Iowa that he depicted is still recognizable today. And, beyond all expectations, Wood's art remains today as relevant as ever.

For much of his short life Wood focused his work on the Iowa of his era, a rural, agricultural state in the slow process of becoming urbanized. His memorable paintings, prints, and drawings of Iowa are a blend of truthful observation and romantic fantasy (some of his more fanciful landscapes prefigure the wildly stylized world of Dr. Seuss). But throughout his work, Wood also dealt with such crucial human issues as community, trust, hope, and history. The period of Wood's mature artwork lasted less than two decades, but nearly everything he did in this brief span was part of an attempt to artistically collate his vision for a more ethical America.

Anyone who visits the twenty-first-century version of Grant Wood's Iowa will find that his biographical and artistic trail leads to museums, university and college campuses, a sprawling and still active religious colony, numerous historic houses (including his original studio), the birthplace of an American president, the home of the governor of Iowa, and the Veteran's Memorial building, where his magnificent stained-glass window is the centerpiece. One can also find here buildings and landscapes that have barely changed over the course of the last century.

The book before you is a wonderful way to launch into your own exploration and appreciation of the work of this son of America's heartland, a true American original, Iowa's beloved Grant Wood.

—TERRY PITTS
Executive Director
Cedar Rapids Museum of Art
and the Grant Wood Studio

PREFACE

As an Iowan, an organic farmer, and an art enthusiast, I must admit that setting out on the road to visit the landmarks of Grant Wood's life was a sort of pilgrimage for me. I have always admired Grant Wood's ability to communicate the psychological tension between the quiet sparseness and overwhelming fertility of my home state. He playfully yet respectfully presents the sensuous, graceful eternity of the land, which always humbles me as an Iowa organic farmer. I likewise feel that I know the intimidating characters in his portraits; they could be my neighbors, these people who are resourceful and enterprising enough to survive any economic crisis or series of floods and blizzards and droughts, but open and trusting enough to leave their homes unlocked—and casually walk into your home at any moment, unannounced!

I moved to Iowa as an adult, and Grant Wood was the first cultural reference point I had for Iowa before I began farming in rural Story County. Now that I've lived in Iowa for a decade, I've determined that Grant Wood has proven a dependable ambassador for the state, because the admiration I had as an outsider for the idealized Iowan landscapes and quirky American characters has held true to my experience as an Iowan farmer. Raising three children on an Iowa farm has been a dream come true after leaving New York City. I wonder if their childhood has been very different from that of Grant Wood's, sharing the same gloriously fecund landscape as a backdrop for imaginative exploration. I pray that their adulthoods will emulate Grant Wood's in that their early foundation in an Iowan culture and ecology will enliven their senses, spirituality, and confidence.

For me, Grant Wood is our poet of place, and insomuch that Iowa is often called upon to represent the emblematic "Heartland" of the United States, he communicates a central theme in the American imagination: to remain innocent while manifesting strength. Grant Wood documents the naive spirit of our nation, which manages to frequently redeem us despite our cultural and historic foibles. The sardonic honesty of Grant Wood's art mimics the frankness of the Iowa people I know, and the luminosity of his art reflects the quiet, radiant spirituality of Iowa that visitors will discover while following this guided tour.

—WENDE ELLIOTT

I have known of Grant Wood since my childhood, though the exact moment when I became aware of his painting *American Gothic* is not certain to me. Grant Wood had somehow written himself indelibly into my personal history of art and was part of my collection of great masters before I was even aware that art history existed.

Until my trip to his native Iowa in the spring of 2010, I had seen very little of his body of work firsthand, or for that matter the places where he lived and worked for the majority of his life. I did not expect very much from my trip in terms of either the place or the culture. I was making my trip for personal rather than cultural reasons.

It has been a genuine surprise and pleasure to come to know both the state of Iowa and the paintings of Grant Wood. Before arriving in Iowa, I flew to Chicago from England and went immediately to the Art Institute to see the collection of American masters, including O'Keeffe, Hopper, and that troubling figure Albright. I scrutinized *American Gothic* with European eyes, finding it richer than the reproductions I had seen of it, and certainly more painterly. It seemed in quality somewhat equivalent to an English painter of roughly the same period, Stanley Spencer.

I was driven to Ames and used it as a base for exploring Iowa. It became immediately apparent to me after visiting the Des Moines Art Center that I should see a lot more of Grant Wood's paintings, that he was an important figure in a place that was growing on me by leaps and bounds.

My reaction to Iowa was unexpected. I did not expect to like the state or to think of it as a place of culture, but I took to the old red barns, to the gentle roll of the farm fields, to the railways, to the old city centers of Dubuque, Cedar Rapids, Iowa City, and Ames, to name just a few features. The old downtown center of Ames moved me immediately, and I wanted to purchase a house on one of its sunny and expansive small-town city blocks with roomy homes and lush green lawns. While I fell for these places and the pleasant ingenuity of the largely anonymous Midwestern architecture, I came to think more and more of Grant Wood, and how in some way he and I saw Iowa in the same light. His vision echoed in all that attracted me to the places I was visiting.

My arrival in Iowa also brought a renewed interest in sustainability, and the state highlighted the difference between a sustainable world and a less sustainable one. I felt that somehow Grant Wood was integral to this notion of sustainability, that he had defined and articulated the character of a place and had seen the things that would be sustainable about Iowa: a type of person, a humane and responsible agriculture, a feeling for nature, a rootedness based in farming, and a small-town friendliness.

Grant Wood was also a pioneer who had created a place for Iowan artists; he had founded a tradition. As a strong painter with a recognizable character, he was an artist who others could look up to not so much for stylistic training, but as an example of dedication, devotion, and determination. Despite Wood's great fame, it remains apparent that his life was not terribly easy, and he suffered the typical financial setbacks associated with his vocation.

My surprise at my reaction to Iowa stemmed from my experience in a very different part of the world. In 1991 I made my first visit to Sansepolcro, Tuscany, in the province of Arezzo, and the area known as the upper Tiber valley. As a painter I was following what John Pope-Hennessy called the trail of Piero della Francesca, which the painter Balthus also followed in the early 1920s. I subsequently settled and painted in this area of Italy and gained a much greater sense of the culture and art of the region.

As I became more aware of Grant Wood and the type of painter and person he was, I started to try to understand him within the context of other artists with whom I was familiar. My sense of his importance was galvanized upon seeing his murals in the library of the Iowa State University in Ames. These made me think of the *Cycle of the True Cross,* painted by Piero della Francesca in Arezzo, and though Wood's murals in no way compete with these works, they do express a very similar kind of career, ambition, and sense of place. I was impressed with their scale, their thoroughness, and their architecture. They are the works of a painter dedicated to the enrichment of a community, and they foster an appreciation for art within that community.

The excellent tour I was given of Grant Wood's studio in Cedar Rapids further acquainted me with aspects of his practices, which I could also relate to that of Piero della Francesca's. Chief among these was his method of working locally and building up a collection of paintings and commissions that served his region. This seems to be fundamental to the notion of sustainability and community, and I believe it is the crucial ingredient in both artists' genius. They were both dedicated to a locality that they wished to embellish and celebrate in the company of friends and family. Such artistic work also seems to be intimately tied to a respect for nature and to ecological agriculture, which is an act of devotion and dedication to a place.

While my initial trip to Iowa was tinged with skepticism, my travels to the state became the expression of a love affair with the places Grant Wood lived and the work he made. Wood's ebullience and sense of humor are apparent in all that I have seen regarding him. *Grant Wood's Iowa* is a sumptuous way of seeing the best of Iowa and, to my mind, a wonderful way of becoming acquainted with a beautiful but somewhat unknown place filled with culture and a natural poetry.

—WILLIAM BALTHAZAR ROSE

ACKNOWLEDGMENTS

A sincere thanks to the curators and registrars of Grant Wood's art, personal writings, and family memorabilia in Cedar Rapids, Des Moines, and Davenport museums: Sean Ulster, Teri VanDorston, Andrew Wallace, Amy Worthen, and Mickey Koch. Thank you to Coe College for its collaboration and to amateur historians Kristy Raines and Cecilia Hatcher. Thank you to Iowa Poet Laureate and ISU professor Mary Swander, who believed in my work and encouraged me to pursue a masters in fine arts despite me being older than many of my professors and the fact I would need to haphazardly learn how to balance on a bicycle while wearing a backpack all over again. A warm thank you to our good-humored, long-suffering editor Kermit Hummel at the Countryman imprint of W. W. Norton.

I thank the farmers, artists, and writers, including Donna Pritizgas, Beth Brockman-Miller, Dalia Hierro, Clemence Enou, Katherine Rupp, Jacqueline Delay-Stockdale, Jennifer Conrad, Namita Devidayal, Gwen Foster, Celia Barbour, Shelley Rogers, Mary Dyer, Martha Norton, and Susan Jasper, for their involvement as spiritual midwives in the birth of this book. Lastly, I offer up my gratitude for my husband, William Balthazar Rose, whom I met in a painting class at Princeton University a quarter of a century ago and encourages me to live artfully still.

—WENDE ELLIOTT

Grant Wood's palette and tools
Image courtesy of the Figge Art Museum, Grant Wood Archive, Davenport, Iowa

HOW TO USE THIS BOOK

This book can be used to plan a weeklong art-appreciation road trip or independent weekend outings, with ancillary attractions that can enjoyably extend a traveler's visit from a four-hour tour into an overnight stay. Alternatively, this book can simply be enjoyed as a bedside art study guide for self-edification.

The format of this book was consciously chosen to not only facilitate a geographical journey across Grant Wood's home state, but also to transport the visitor chronologically, psychologically, and culturally across the landscape and events that affected Wood's work. While a reader can move through the book's sites geographically by starting in Davenport, at the eastern border of Iowa on the Mississippi River, and then wending westward, one can instead start chronologically in Anamosa, Grant Wood's birthplace and burial place. From there the reader can tour the Cedar Rapids of Wood's boyhood; drive back toward Stone City, the locus of his adult artist-colony years; venture west to Ames, recalling his professional pinnacle as director of the Public Works of Art Project (PWAP); then circle back to Iowa City, a half hour due south of Cedar Rapids, where in his last years he struggled to fit into the roles of husband and academic. Additional stops in Davenport and Des Moines are suggested because of their fine art museums with Regionalist artwork and contemporary cultural scenes, but they are not places where Grant Wood lived.

The first two parts of this book explore his early childhood, the buildings he knew, and the schools he attended. Sites such as these that are directly related to Grant Wood's life and his art are labeled with the 🌿 icon. Other sites aim to acquaint the traveler with the Iowan landscapes, buildings, and people of Grant Wood's time, which are labeled with the 🌾 icon. Lastly, several sites are included that feature local artwork other than Grant Wood's, and these are labeled with the 🐾 icon.

Each chapter has a special section called "Today's Landscape," where one is directed to current cultural and ecological attractions so trips are not only educational, but also contemporary. These include nature hikes and parks where one can enjoy the landscapes immortalized by Wood, annual special events and festivals, driving tours, contemporary local artists' studios, and more. Since a commitment to purchasing local seasonal organic ingredients and the slow food movement have a toehold in Iowa, farmer's markets, wineries, and agritourism sites have also been listed. The agricultural themes of Grant Wood's paintings can be best appreciated by meeting Iowa farmers, and then you will understand better why Wood decided to make farmer's bib overalls his signature style and a show of Iowa allegiance. As Grant Wood was an amateur thespian (photos survive of him in costume with his friends in the Society for the Prevention of Cruelty to Speakers club), current performing-arts venues are also included. Consider supporting the local contemporary art scene by enjoying the performing arts and buying a piece of regional art as a souvenir of your adventure in Grant Wood's Iowa.

More information about hikes and camping options in Iowa's breathtaking terrain can be found online at www.traveliowa.com. A comprehensive list of accommodations can be found online at the Iowa Bed and Breakfast Guild, www.ibbg.com.

If touring Grant Wood's Iowa has whet your appetite and you have more time, parts 3 and 5 also include "Farther Afield" sections, in which additional sites of interest that are a bit farther away are featured.

By traversing the same roads, viewing the same landscapes, and enjoying the same sunsets that Grant Wood experienced, the traveler will gain a better understanding of Wood's life and the ideas that informed his art—and the art of other Regionalists. The art created through his example has greatly enhanced the lives of many Iowans, and it is but a portion of the tremendous talent that the state has to offer.

Grant Wood and Thomas Hart Benton pose in costume as representatives of the Society for the Prevention of Cruelty to Speakers club, 1935. Image courtesy of the Figge Art Museum, Grant Wood Archive, Davenport, Iowa

I C O N   K E Y

Sites directly related to Grant Wood's life and his art

Iowan landscapes, buildings, and people of Grant Wood's time

Sites that feature local artwork other than Grant Wood's

Study for Self-Portrait *(1932), Grant Wood*
Charcoal and pastel on paper, 14½ x 12¾ in. Museum
purchase. 93.11. Cedar Rapids Museum of Art

GRANT WOOD

Tormented Hero of the Heartland

*About once in each generation, directed by political or
economic or artistic impulses, we have re-evaluated
or reinterpreted ourselves.*

—GRANT WOOD

America is made up of heroes, known and unknown, real heroes, tragic heroes, and false ones. Grant Wood is without doubt an American hero. He managed to overcome numerous obstacles and leave a lasting legacy for other artists and for all those seeking a defining light in a state with little or no previous cultural history. His story is, however, all too human and reveals a person of mixed talents with a complex and at times difficult personality.

His fame is largely based on one painting, *American Gothic*. It is a simple, meticulous, and almost menacing portrait of a man and a woman standing in front of a white timber house built in the Carpenter Gothic style. It is one of American art's most memorable paintings and is immediately recalled by a majority of Americans at the mere mention of its title. This one painting has become indelibly engraved in the mind's eye. It is one of the great precursors of pop art, having been reproduced and interpreted to such an extent that its familiarity is akin to that of Kellogg's Rice Krispies or Mount Rushmore.

*Citizens at a grocery store at the time
of Grant Wood's birth*
Anamosa Historic Society

The creator of this painting came from humble Victorian origins. He was born in 1891 on a farm south of the small quarry town of Anamosa, to Hattie Weaver and Francis Maryville Wood. His father was a strict industrious man of Quaker upbringing, and his mother had been a schoolteacher. Both were the first-born children of fairly prosperous families who had come from the Northeast during the first decades of settlement in Iowa. They met at the local Presbyterian church, where Hattie played the organ and Francis was a Sunday school teacher, and married in 1886, when Francis was 30 and Hattie 26. Grant had three siblings: Frank, born in

Downtown Anamosa at time of Grant Wood's birth   Anamosa Historic Society

1886; John, born in 1893; and Nan, born in 1899. Grant received a rudimentary education in a one-room schoolhouse and had a strong fondness for his farm animals, raising chickens, ducks, and turkeys.

Very early on, Grant began to draw, and he was encouraged by his mother, who gave him cardboard from old boxes and charcoaled twigs as art supplies. Gruff and critical, his father was judgmental of Grant's predilection for art and found it effeminate and passive compared to farming. His mother compensated for this by hiding him under the kitchen table so he could continue his drawings. Wood lived with his mother, who supported and nurtured his talent throughout her lifetime, for most of his life, and the two were largely inseparable until her death.

After his father's death in 1901, when Grant was 10, the family moved to the prosperous town of Cedar Rapids, which became the locus of Wood's life and creativity for many years. It was in Cedar Rapids that he acquired lifelong friends and patrons, where he was educated and became an educator himself, and where he painted his most important and celebrated works.

Cedar Rapids is an essential place in the understanding of Grant Wood, and, fortunately enough for those following in the Grant Wood pilgrimage, much of it exists as it did in his time. Wood used the town as a base throughout his life, leaving and returning to it and to his family. His first major foray away from Cedar Rapids was to study art at the Minneapolis School of Design and Handicraft in 1910.

Wood studied art in high school but had developed very early (before the age of 10) the ambition of being an illustrator. This is part of what made him so remarkable; his foresight in knowing his future vocation, and his innate sense of having a destiny at such a young age. In fact, a photo taken of him in 1910, when he was 19, shows him garbed in an artist's smock and holding a palette as he stands in front of an easel, looking every bit an accomplished artist.

His education as an artist seems to have been quite extensive, though it was rather intermittent and piecemeal. He was without a principal mentor, though he was attracted to the theories of Ernest Batchelder, an architect and theoretician who espoused ideas concerning the Arts and Crafts movement. He was briefly a student of Batchelder's when he studied drawing at the Art Institute of Chicago from 1913 to 1915, and Batchelder's ideas greatly influenced the cherubic Wood. One can see in his career a continual response to the notions of the Arts and Crafts movement: Wood was no mere easel painter, but a dynamic inventor and a playful exponent of the decorative arts. He studied far and wide, immersing himself in as many didactic situations as possible, and as a result his own work reveals the search of a true artist attempting to find his own authentic voice.

In fact, Wood made several valiant efforts to educate himself. The adventurous, open-minded, and determined Wood endeavored to transcend his provincial roots and see the world. To this end, he set out for the Paris, the mecca of artists before the Second World War, in 1920 at the age of 29 with his high school friend Marvin Cone. It was the first of several trips. They were late bloomers and distinctly out of fashion in the City of Light. It seems clear from the vantage of almost a hundred years hence that Grant and his friend must have appeared like country bumpkins to the sophisticated tastes of the French and international avant-garde, and yet the experience must have marked indelibly on Wood's ego the desire to measure up—which he most certainly did when he entered the world stage with the creation of *American Gothic* in 1930 at the age of 39.

The effects of contemporary European art of the period seem hardly to appear in his work, and there is almost no name-dropping in regards to famous artists he could have encountered in Paris at the time, such as Picasso and Chagall. Instead, the effects of Paris on Wood's painting were to bring out an impressionist style, which helped to make a claim for him back in Iowa but was hopelessly retrograde to the European avant-garde.

Grant Wood as a young artist, 1910   Cedar Rapids Museum of Art Archives

In his second of three trips to Paris, he was briefly enrolled in the Academie Julien in 1923, a famous stop for American artists. There he seems to have been ridiculed and was given the nickname *tete de bois,* or "wooden head," a rather clever take on his last name, however unpleasant he may have found it.

Despite this, Wood did not have an ideal education as an artist, partly as it seemed that he had to support himself, working odd jobs and enrolling in night school. There was almost nothing to suggest that he should become anything more than an average artist; he did not become associated with any of the major artists while studying abroad, nor did he come from the type of family that could assist him financially. His skill was also not of a spectacular order, and his origins in a backwater rural community were not altogether

Grant Wood made many self-portraits, including this one, cast in brass in 1925. Self-Portrait, ca. 1925, brass, 3 x 2 x 1 in. Gift of Harriet Y. and John B. Turner II. 72.12.59. Cedar Rapids Museum of Art

promising, either. Great artists have long been associated with prominent cities and celebrated artistic dynasties—nothing the state of Iowa could easily afford to claim. Yet it was the state of Iowa that offered him a constant home and a sense of his roots when his wanderlust dried up, and it also provided the inspiration for his work.

Indeed, it was the temperament of the state, with its simple citizens and lack of grandeur, that helped to forge the truly remarkable genius of this quirky, irascible, and at times tormented artist, an artist who produced images more penetrating than the iconic paintings of pop artists decades later. A rival to the cultural importance of Chicago, Iowa is both more mysterious and poetic than Illinois and can claim to be the birthplace of this visionary spokesman and grandfather of pop art.

In Wood's earlier years, circumstances often dictated that he had to turn his hand to things other than painting in order to earn a living, and he took on the role as the head of the family, acting as almost a surrogate husband and father after his brothers moved away. Not an easy thing to do for an artist! He assisted his mother and his sister on a continual basis, often providing accommodation and money. To this end, he was involved in speculative building and also briefly had a metalworking business in Chicago. He taught in the local school system for a long period after the war, but he did not achieve a more prestigious academic position until after he became famous, the University of Iowa employed him.

Wood was not a tall man. His numerous self-portraits and photos of him suggest he verged on the plump side, wore glasses most of the time, had a cleft chin, and had closely cropped hair reminiscent of his time spent in the army from 1918 to 1919, when he was stationed at Camp Dodge outside of Des Moines. During this period he went to Washington to design camouflage and sculpt models for artillery equipment. Later he wore his military uniform to the school where taught in Cedar Rapids in order to save money.

He had the idiosyncratic habit of bobbing from side to side when he spoke. There was an element of mirth to him, though at times this meant he was considered a sort of town fool and a "character" in Cedar Rapids. His style of dress, including his penchant for wearing workman's overalls, contributed to this view of him. While this distinguished him from other painters, it also reinforced his allegiance with the farmer and his rural origins. The apparition of a goatee he had grown in Paris, evidence of the bohemian lifestyle he emulated, was so lampooned by the locals that he shaved it off soon after his return to Iowa.

As a student, Wood worked odd jobs, including that of a mortuary assistant. He famously joked about nailing on a corpse's toupee when it kept falling off, and for this offense he was reportedly sacked. This little story is far from irrelevant; the mortuary world was a recurring theme in his life. The studio-home where he lived in Cedar Rapids belonged to no other than his most major patron, David Turner of Turner Mortuary, and it was located next door to the mortuary. Wood lived there for over 10 years, and during that time he must have witnessed the commerce of corpses and mourning families coming and going.

Five Turner Alley, as Wood called his studio, was on the upper floor of the Turner Mortuary carriage house. It was offered to him in 1924 by the Turners and was to become the birthplace of some of America's most famous paintings. With its view of the mortuary from the window, it must have been a strange, sad place in which to dredge up inspiration and create some of the most renowned works of American 20th-century painting. Perhaps this proximity to the funereal world can partially account for the somewhat ironic, severe, and overtly penetrating aspects of Wood's output.

In exchange for rent, he provided paintings to the Turners. David Turner knew these paintings would be worth huge sums someday. Wood's studio had to house himself as well as his mother and sister, and it had little or no privacy and gave infrequent escape from the somewhat overwhelming fumes of the oil paint. Yet it remains today the worthy monument of a great American painter, where one can almost smell the aroma of lunch merging with the scent of oil paint and hear the echo of the breath of this long-deceased and eccentric genius.

One example of Wood's wide range of skills and interests, and a byproduct of his need to diversify in order to earn a living, is the Veterans Memorial stained-glass window in the Veterans Memorial Building in Cedar Rapids. This spectacular project led to Wood's last trip to Europe in 1928, when he traveled to Munich to oversee the construction of the stained glass.

In Germany he was influenced by medieval German and Flemish artists—such as Albrecht Dürer, Hans Holbein, and

Dunn Funeral Home Patio (*n.d.*), *Grant Wood.*
His experience with and proximity to funeral homes was evident in Wood's work.
28 x 24 in., oil on canvas. Des Moines Art Center Permanent Collections; Bequest of Martha Dunn Trump in memory of LeRoy C. Dunn, 2002.30. Photo: Ray Andrews

Hans Memling—as well as contemporary German artists of the Neue Sachlichkeit (New Objectivity) movement, which transformed his art. He abandoned the impressionistic style he had developed in Paris and began to make paintings of a much tighter and clearly drawn order, painted smoothly and unrelenting in their realistic rendition of life. Perhaps the first painting to truly express this transformation is *Woman with Plants,* a portrait Wood painted of his mother upon his return to Cedar Rapids. This stylistic transformation provided Wood the necessary technique to realize his vision. With its strong leaning on the traditional craft of picture making, it seemed quite contrary to most contemporary trends, yet in Wood's hands it would contribute to some of the most iconic American paintings of the first half of the 20th century.

Wood began a series of portraits in this new style, one of which was a double portrait. His subjects were his sister and his dentist, posed in front of a rather unusual building he had noticed in the small town of Eldon when he had conducted an art class there as a visiting teacher. The finished painting, which many assume is of a married couple (but was intended to be a father with his spinster daughter), has captured the imagination of people throughout the world. He entitled it *American Gothic.*

The creation and subsequent meteoric rise to fame of *American Gothic* changed Wood's life forever. The bittersweet story is that the painting of the then-unknown Grant Wood was submitted to a juried competition at the Art Institute of Chicago and then purchased by the institute for $300. This price was later to seem ridiculously low, and Wood was greatly offended when he thought of the obscene profit the museum must have gained from the painting. However, it ushered Wood into the realm of the successful, and he was courted by wealthy collectors, asked to give lecture tours, invited to present exhibitions in New York, and, most prestigiously of all, appointed the director of the Public Works of Art Project (PWAP) for the state of Iowa.

Despite all this, what was truly a triumph for Wood was the creation of a unique vision and sensibility that drew attention to his provincial roots and celebrated them. There was something about Iowa that spoke *big* to the world at large, that challenged the supremacy of the East Coast and Parisian art worlds. This was during the Depression, a time when there was a call for a more sensible, back to basics thinking, and Wood, a humanist who brought to life the common man and the Heartland, a man whose art represented American values in a simple and unpretentious way, was celebrated.

This success and growing fame led to a clarifying of Wood's vision, and he immersed himself in all sorts of projects: a memoir entitled *Return from Bohemia;* a short essay, *Revolt Against the City;* illustrations for a book called *Main Street* by Sinclair Lewis, which was based on the Midwest; mural projects for Iowa State University; lithographs, landscapes, historical paintings, and portraits; lectures; the formation of an art colony; and a directorship. What a busy man!

All this helped to advance Wood and his role in what has come to be known as Regionalism, American Regionalism, and even Midwestern Regionalism. As Wood became more successful, he associated with larger cultural figures, forming friendships with other Midwestern artists including Thomas Hart Benton and John Steuart Curry, and this group very loosely made up a sort of school of art with a philosophy. To its exponents Regionalism expressed the values of rural small-town life and offered serious art based on the principals of drawing with a realistic approach. It also attempted to enliven local communities and provide cultural stimulation in them by fostering art. To this extent it was a grassroots, humanist, nature-based agrarian art movement. Their

John Steuart Curry (left) and Grant Wood, two pioneers of the Regionalist art movement, at Stone City, 1933. Cedar Rapids Museum of Art. Photo: John W. Barry. 89.2.16

growing recognition must have been perceived as a sort of victory against the domination of the East Coast art establishment, a victory similar to that of David over Goliath. This success was short-lived, however, and all to soon Midwestern art, and Grant Wood and *American Gothic,* were considered narrow-minded, politically regressive, backward, and provincial.

Fame and success did not benefit Wood's character, and he became intolerant and difficult. He may have also seemed slightly paranoid, allowing his position as a painter to become rather too political and authoritarian. However, this does not discount Wood's role as a hero, albeit a tragic one. As an artist he was an underdog, a speaker for the valiant and struggling masses, but as a man his later years brought bad fortune. His painful marriage late in life to a woman who in no way sheltered or supported him led to a quick divorce, and not long after, in 1942, he died of cancer at the age of 50.

His personal life has been the object of continual inquisition, with suggestions of sexual deviance and repression. The climate of the Midwest of his time did not allow for sexual experimentation, and the strict covenants of marriage went against the grain of many bohemian artists. There is also the suggestion of a deep feeling of inadequacy in his work, the inadequacy of a provincial spokesman for a class of people forsaken by the posh and cultivated world who could never quite achieve the desired level of sophistication.

His paintings go a long way to address this imbalance and to suggest the gentle irony of the Midwestern temperament. Wood's vast iconic repertoire and its definitive presence resonate loudly in the world of art, vehemently suggesting the vision of a society with such succinct articulation that one begins to wonder whether it is places like Cedar Rapids that are the truest cultural centers.

The Horsetraders (Two Horsetraders, *1918*), *Grant Wood*
Oil on composition board, 11 x 14 in., Gift of Harriet Y. and John B Turner II.
72.12.28. Cedar Rapids Museum of Art

1 ANAMOSA AND STONE CITY

The Place of Origin and Return

In my own private world, Anamosa
was as important as Europe was to
Columbus, and the Wapsie Valley—
a half-dozen miles from our farm—
had all the glamour that the Orient
had for Magellan and Vespucci.
                              —GRANT WOOD

Grant **Wood** remains a widely recognized but narrowly understood icon of American culture. His reputation has been one of extremes: The Midwestern populace cherishes him as a heroic figure who began life as an ordinary farm child and rose to national fame celebrating the common man, while art critics have dismissed him for his antimodernist views and sentimental illustrative style. Bordered to the east by Illinois, the state claiming Abraham Lincoln, and to the south by Missouri, home state of Mark Twain, Iowa has chosen Grant Wood to fill the spot of the homeboy who didn't shun his roots and instead forced the world to take him and Iowa seriously.

His Victorian rural childhood made a lasting impact on the subject matter of his art. Grant Wood was born in 1891 on a farm south of Anamosa, which no longer exists. He lived there until the age of 10, when his father died, at which time the family moved to Cedar Rapids. Anamosa, located 25 miles north of Cedar Rapids, is today a town of 2,000 people. In an autobiography Wood left unfinished at the time of his death, he recollected enjoying country fairs, buggy excursions, church socials, and simple gift exchanges at Christmastime. Curiously, he developed writer's block when he

Anamosa, as it looks today. It's been seemingly unchanged by time. Anamosa Chamber of Commerce

came to the point of the narrative when his father died and his family left their farm.

The village is proud of Grant Wood's legacy and hosts an annual Grant Wood art festival, offers a Grant Wood visitors center that is open year-round, and maintains his gravesite and the one-room schoolhouse where he attended school. These sites illustrate the rural world he knew, with its turn-of-the-20th-century small-town rituals and values, which is deeply routed in Wood's agrarian identity.

If you'd like to see the site of the Wood family farmstead, you can drive past it on Grant Wood Road off IA 64. IA 64 starts at the junction of US 151 at the edge of town. Turn east on 64, heading toward Amber. Turn left on the second gravel road, labeled Grant Wood Road. The visual marker for finding the intersection nearest the farm site is the former county nursing home. Before reaching it, look for the fancy cement fence posts that remain from a prior fence. The farmstead was here. It is past the second farmstead but before the county nursing home. It is startling to see just how efficiently nature can erase all trace of man and man-made structures.

Although there is not much left to see here, it can be helpful to visit this site to orient oneself with the agrarian landscape of Wood's young imagination. The crops of surrounding farm fields typically rotate annually from dense, dark bushes of soybeans to vigorous corn ("knee high by the fourth of July"), to oats that mature to a rosy amber by midsummer, and to alfalfa cut for dairy and beef cattle. At the former county nursing home, poor local residents were allowed to live in old age. The civic spirit of the farming community to care for its least fortunate residents with such safety nets as a communal working farm and nursing care facility is typical of the era Wood lived in, before there were nationalized welfare programs. Abandoned county nursing homes still dot the Iowa countryside today.

For more information about the area, contact the Jones County Tourism Association, 120 E. Main Street, Anamosa, 319-462-4104 or 800-383-0831; or Grant Wood Gallery and Visitor Center, 124 E. Main Street, Anamosa, 319-462-4267, www.grantwoodartgallery.org.

Feeding the Chickens (1917–1918), *Grant Wood* 11 x 14 in., oil on composition board.
Gift of Harriet Y. and John B Turner II. 72.12.20. Cedar Rapids Museum of Art

 # ANTIOCH ONE-ROOM SCHOOLHOUSE
4 miles east of Anamosa on IA 64

Founded in 1872, the one-room schoolhouse where Grant Wood began his education is lovingly maintained by the local volunteers of the Paint and Palette Club after the school board deeded the building to the society in honor of Wood. The interior is not yet restored, so the stop will be primarily for a photo opportunity and picnic spot if you wish. Grant Wood and his siblings attended the school from 1897 to 1901. His sister, Nan, wrote this about his school memories: "When Grant was a young boy, each day as he meandered from his farm home to school, he observed the wonders around him—the plowed fields, the growing corn, the seasons of the year, the animals of the field, the people, and the little country school he attended called Antioch. These scenes of his childhood made a lasting impression on him, and in later years, he immortalized them in such paintings as *Young Corn, Fall Plowing, Spring Turning,* and *Dinner for Threshers.*"

Graduates of the school recount how a potbellied stove stood in the center of the room, how the teacher would board at a family's farm, and how the students would rush home from school to change clothes, fill the wood box,

The Antioch One-Room Schoolhouse is where Grant Wood began his education. Anamosa Chamber of Commerce

shuck corn, milk cows, feed hogs, and take horses out to drink, then go to bed early and get up early again.

Ten-year-old student Zella Johnson wrote the school song, "Our School," to the tune of "Yankee Doodle Dandy":

The boys and girls of Antioch
are very fond of learning,
So many come to fill the room—
there's hardly chance for turning.

Chorus:
Oh! Don't you think we are very smart
to learn our lessons all by heart,
Every scholar does his part
and that's the way we learn, sir!

GW GRANT WOOD GALLERY AND VISITOR CENTER

124 E. Main St., Anamosa   *www.grantwoodartgallery.org*
319-462-4267   *Open 1–4 daily*

Right on **Main Street,** this Victorian storefront is loaded with all types of odds and ends of the purchasable variety, from Grant Wood church cookbooks to prairie planting guides. Staffed by effusive elderly volunteers from the community, the place is pervaded by a dustiness that may not have been cleared since Grant Wood's last visit. There is an extensive collection of parodies of *American Gothic* plastered on the walls and a version of that painting with the faces cut out so you and your traveling companion can replace the homely couple's mugs with your own delightful visages. With all the folksiness of a small-town antiques shop, here you can set a relaxed, whimsical tone for the rest of your road trip.

The Grant Wood Gallery and Visitor Center William Balthazar Rose

ABOVE: *You can pose for your own* American Gothic*–style photo at the visitors center.*

LEFT: *Life-size versions of the figures in* American Gothic Both by William Balthazar Rose

ANAMOSA STATE PENITENTIARY

Anamosa Penitentiary Museum
N. High St., Anamosa
319-462-2386
www.asphistory.com/museum

Open noon–4 Fri.–Sun., May–Oct.,
or by appointment
Admission: $3

The Anamosa State Penitentiary probably always has been, and always will be, the most imposing presence and piece of architecture in the town of Anamosa. Established in 1875, the penitentiary towers over the rest of the town like a Gothic fortress. The largest building in Jones County, the Victorian-era prison still incarcerates over one thousand inmates. The Anamosa State Penitentiary Museum, housed just outside the prison's walls in its former cheese-making barn, has a gift shop and changing exhibits on the construction of the imposing structure, the history of prison guards, and other topics that you may find helpful to include in your holiday conversations if you happen to be chaperoning belligerent children who need a reminder of what will happen should they make some really bad choices.

The presence of the inmates in such a small town must have made a major impression on the families in the village during the time of Grant Wood's upbringing. In the 19th century, inmates worked in the rock quarries at nearby Stone City, and the remnants of this work are immortalized in Grant Wood's painting *Stone City, Iowa,* which is on display at the Joslyn Art Museum in

*The imposing edifice of the Anamosa
Penitentiary* William Balthazar Rose

Omaha (see "Farther Afield" in part 5). The art colony Grant founded in Stone City in the deserted buildings of the former mining town has a clear view of the quarries, which were manned by forced labor, and the extravagant stone architecture of Stone City was only possible due to the financial profits achieved from the prison workforce. It is interesting to contemplate how Grant Wood chose this mining town and former work camp as a spot for his free-thinking artist commune, and to what extent the themes of artistic and personal freedom were meditations for him. The inmates still work inside the prison, and today Iowa Prison Industries produces metal stamping, metal furniture, road signs, cleaning products, and custom woodwork. The penitentiary also offers the inmates vocational training and certificates in horticulture, auto repair, welding, and janitorial services.

 RIVERSIDE CEMETERY

S. Elm St., Anamosa
319-462-6055 (City
Administration)
http://iowagravestones.org/
cemetery_list.php?CID=
53&cName=Riverside

*Open daylight hours daily,
year-round*

G rant Wood's tombstone is hard to find, much like searching for a needle in a haystack, first due to the modesty of the marker and second due to the cemetery's decision to keep the site discreet without readily obvious signage. The small humble tombstone is flush with the grass, next to his mother's. A short distance away, there is a life-size lion on a

*The entrance to Riverside Cemetery
acknowledges its famous resident.*
William Balthazar Rose

The approach to the Wood plot from the lane is lovely in autumn.

large family marker that reads WOOD, but this is not Grant Wood's tombstone.

In the event the visitors center cannot give you detailed directions to the tombstone, here is how to find it: Enter the cemetery, proceeding straight until you reach the back. Turn left, wrapping around the hill. Look for the lion marker on your left. Wood's tomb is before this large family marker.

You can go on a cemetery tour in Rome and visit the tombstone of John Keats or make a pilgrimage to Graceland to see the resting place of Elvis, but being completely alone in the silence of a small-town cemetery with golden autumnal leaves covering the lawn is greatly moving, when you realize it is the resting place of such a world renowned artist as Grant Wood.

Grant Wood's modest tombstone.
William Balthazar Rose

STONE CITY ART COLONY

*Jones County Tourism
Association
120 E. Main St., Anamosa*

*319-462-4101 or
800-383-0831*

About five miles west of Anamosa, Stone City is situated on the steep
banks of the Wapsipinicon River and was a prosperous limestone quarry
town before the invention of Portland cement, after which the quarry was
abandoned. The community was founded in 1850, and at the economic height
of settlement in 1896, 10 quarries were in production. The quarries were the
first in the United States known to use hydraulic power. The 500-person population was supplemented by forced labor from the Anamosa State Penitentiary (see page 5), who were "reformed" in part by their work in the quarries.
The self-financed company town at one time had an opera house that featured
top-billed vaudeville acts like Tom Thumb and Jenny Lind, a railway station,
a post office, a schoolhouse, a blacksmith shop, a water tower, and several
private homes—all grandiose and built of limestone. Turn-of-the-20th-century
quarry owner J. A. Green built a 12-room stone mansion that was later used
as the main building for the art school and artist colony that Wood established
here in the summer of 1932.

Grant Wood was joined by his high school friend Marvin Cone and other
colleagues in this venture, a risky and foolhardy one as they had no financial
backing and the nation was in the midst of the Great Depression. However,
Wood yearned to return to his roots and re-create his childhood. In some ways,

Old Quarry, Stone City *(1963), Marvin Cone*   George T. Henry College Archives, Stewart Memorial
Library, Coe College

Art Insight: The Roots of Regionalism

Primarily a Midwestern art movement that sought to portray local stories, local landscapes, and local heroes, Regionalism's exponents were occupied with rural life and American culture. Grant Wood believed that Regionalism was a modern art movement that gave roots and identity to the American artist, and his views have often been considered a bit reactionary.

Regionalism, in its attempt to substantiate local artists and everyday life, developed during (and perhaps because of) the Great Depression. Many Regionalist artists had been trained in the Arts and Crafts movement, which was led by William Morris and others in England before World War I. Political ideas of equality and socialism fed their artistic impetus, as well as ideals of hand workmanship being pleasurable and worth maintaining in an increasingly industrialized and automated world. Regionalist artists included Grant Wood, Thomas Hart Benton, John Steuart Curry, Isabel and John Bloom, Marvin Cone, George Rickey, Arnold Pyle, Lowell Hauser, and Christian Petersen, as well as writers such as Sinclair Lewis, for whom Grant Wood illustrated *Main Street.*

Regionalism has roots in American art, stemming from the Hudson River School painters. It was essentially a movement that was provincial, advocating local artists, and it aimed to celebrate small-town and rural life primarily through realistic techniques of making art. Rejecting East Coast and European art, Wood and his compatriots instead strove to develop an indigenous American art much in the way the abstract expressionists did in the 1950s. The farms and the history of the Midwest inspired them, and creating art that evoked local history and native issues was their aim, rather than the emulation of European art. The Regionalist vision was largely antiurban and antiabstract.

By the time of the Depression in the 1930s, Regionalism was the unofficial style of the Works Progress Administration (WPA), with a huge number of artists painting rural scenes and public murals in post offices and federal buildings. The Public Works of Art Project (PWAP) from 1933 to 1934 promoted Grant Wood to head a large number of artists in the creation of murals in Iowa. However, by the 1940s governmental sponsorship of regional art became suspect by younger art critics and academics because fascist and communist countries used the same kind of realistic art as propaganda.

his interest in revisiting the places he loved during his childhood mirrors the great French postimpressionist painter Cézanne's attraction to Aix-en-Provence. Grant also admired concurrent artist initiatives in Woodstock, New York, and Taos, New Mexico, and so wanted to found an art colony for Midwestern artists who could only afford to travel regionally.

Initial musings of the concept happened in sleepy Eldon, Iowa, where Wood had been invited to teach a community art class en plein air for a few sessions by Harvard academic Edward Rowan in 1929. Rowan ended up participating in the Stone City colony, and once it was established in 1932, he, Wood, and Adrian Dornbush (former director of the Flint Institute of Arts in Michigan and at the time an art instructor at Cedar Rapids's Little Gallery) donated their time to the project without payment, thus attracting matching grant funds from the Carnegie Foundation to the tune of $1,000. Rowan and Dornbush contacted other prominent artists in the Midwest to complete the faculty roster, and local artists volunteered their time. Coe College agreed to grant official course credits for the art classes, and several artists worked together to convert a limestone mansion into classrooms and dormitory. The icehouse became the exhibition gallery, and donated horse-drawn ice wagons became mobile residences for the artists. The colony hosted up to 50 artists at a time, and Sunday public exhibitions would draw hundreds of people, who would pay a dime to see the art and mingle with the colony residents while enjoying a chicken picnic dinner. Despite this, like many utopian ventures, the colony was short-lived and survived only two summers.

Stone City Art Colony faculty, summer of 1932. Grant Wood is near the center, wearing overalls. Cedar Rapids Museum of Art Archives. Photo: John W. Barry

In addition to Wood, Rowan, and Dornbush, colony instructors included Arnold Pyle, a painter and Rowan's assistant at the Little Gallery, who served as framing designer and instructor; David McCosh, an instructor at the Art Institute of Chicago, who taught painting and lithography during the 1932 session; Francis Chapin, a lithography instructor from the Art Institute of Chicago, who taught lithography during the 1933 session; Florence Sprague, an art professor from Drake University in Des Moines, who served as sculpture instructor and held her classes at one of the abandoned quarries; and Marvin Cone, art professor at Coe College and close friend of Wood, who taught figure drawing. The group's mission for the art colony was "to join in working together toward the development of an indigenous expression. To this end, we do not strive for any particular formula or technique. We rather seek for a stimulating exchange of ideas, a cooperation of a variety of points of view."

Tuition ranged from $15 for a two-week commitment to $36 for the entire summer. Women paid $1.50 a week to live on the third floor of the Green Mansion, which was billed as the dormitory. Male students had the option to camp nearby or live in one of the 14 refurbished ice wagons, arranged in a clear line from the mansion to the old stone tower. Newly painted landscapes, cloth awnings, and flower boxes adorned the wagons. Grant Wood chose to live in an ice wagon during his colony stay and is said to have frequently shared his sleeping space with other male students. Students had classes in the morning and afternoons, and ate meals together at a large dining table. Since the mansion lacked elec-

Old ice wagons were used for student and faculty housing at Stone City. Stone City Art Colony, 1932–33. Cedar Rapids Museum of Art. Photo: John W. Barry. 89.2.16.

tricity, evenings were often spent outdoors with music, song, and lectures. The group also renovated the cellar storeroom of the Green Mansion into a rathskeller-style bar named the Sickle and Sheaf.

Wood's leadership style was criticized. Instructor David McCosh resigned, citing his distaste for how the students produced "little Woods," and student Francis Robert White sparked a small revolt and broke with the colony, taking students with him who would later form the Cooperative Mural Painters Group. (This group would paint the Works Progress Administration–sponsored mural at the Cedar Rapids federal courthouse, a controversial project that was later destroyed via a court order.) In Wood's utopia, there was an explicit dedication to artistic exploration, but also to a more bohemian lifestyle, with insinuations of sexual adventure in the ice wagon sleeping arrangements. However, one must really look at his vision as stemming from an Arts and Crafts ideology originating in England, which itself had artistic leadership with formal affiliations to the socialist party in Europe.

After the artistic experiment ended in 1933 due to lack of financial solvency, the ice wagons became chicken coops for local farmers. The property was turned over to financiers as part of the debt settlement, and the Green Mansion was eventually destroyed in a tragic November 1963 fire. Today, many of the buildings have been lost to decay or are occupied as private property, and none of the painted ice wagons are known to still exist. The most striking building that does remain, however, is the stone water tower, a circular medieval-looking stone construction that has an incongruous sense of Camelot. It's on top of the highest hill. The art students called it Adrian's Tomb because instructor Adrian Dornbush chose to sleep there and had to

ABOVE: *This medieval-looking ruined water tower was nicknamed Adrian's Tomb after the Stone City professor who bunked there.*

LEFT: *A replica of the facade of the* American Gothic *house stands at Stone City.* Photos by William Balthazar Rose

ascend to his quarters in the emptied water tank via a ladder.

Across the street from the tower is a replica of the facade of the Eldon house painted by Grant Wood in *American Gothic*. Feel free to pose in front of it for photos. Amusingly, the local rural electric company has painted an homage to Grant Wood on their relay center. The "amped-up" Gothic couple is a fine piece of folk art by a local artist. The electric station is adjacent to the ruins of the amphitheater where Wood's cohorts would perform for each other and at Sunday open houses for the public.

Wood held his classes outdoors, along the bluffs overlooking the river

American Gothic—electrified and amped up! William Balthazar Rose

valley. In his commitment to communicate an "American" style of art, Wood instructed the students of the art colony to use the local scenery and to "find promise in their own regions." To get a sense of this scenery and see the vista that Grant Wood painted in *Stone City, Iowa* in 1932, stand at the top of the hill on US 151 just after passing the replica facade of the *American Gothic* home. Parking is available beside the road at the house facade.

A group working outdoors at the Stone City Art Colony, 1932–1933. Featured are Marvin Cone (at easel) and Adrian Dornbush. Seated between them is Marjorie Nuhn. To Nuhn's left is Persis Weaver Robertson. On Robertson's left is Lela Powers Briggs, a 1933 colony student who was visiting Nuhn at Stone City.
Cedar Rapids Museum of Art. Photo: John W. Barry. 89.2.12

As the summer of 1933 came to an end, Grant Wood was appointed professor in the art department of the University of Iowa, starting a new chapter in his life (which is described in part 3).

TODAY'S LANDSCAPE
Ancillary Art and Ecoattractions

Wapsipinicon State Park

21301 County Road E34, Anamosa
319-462-2761 or 877-427-2757
(to reserve a campsite at any Iowa state park)
www.iowadnr.gov/Destinations/ StateParksRecAreas.aspx
Open daylight hours daily, year-round
Admission: free

Grant Wood spent many hours of his boyhood playing here, in Wapsipinicon Park.
Anamosa Chamber of Commerce

Four-hundred-acre **Wapsipinicon State Park** is a lovely setting for a picnic. The park includes river access and two caves (Horse Thief Cave at one time was used to hide stolen horses).

In his unfinished memoir, Grant Wood recalled his boyhood outings to the Wapsipinicon River valley as feeling as adventurous as ocean crossings from his frame of reference, being a landlocked farm boy. His biographer Park Rinard recorded him saying, "In my own private world, Anamosa was as important as Europe was to Columbus, and the Wapsie Valley, a half-dozen miles from our farm, had all the glamour that the Orient had for Magellan and Vespucci."

Grant Wood Scenic Byway

http://iowadot.gov/iowasbyways

The local tourism boards have organized a country drive that will remind you of Grant Wood's landscapes as you wend your way through several small towns and past rolling farmland dotted with stone buildings, wooden barns, hayfields, and rows of corn. It is also an alternative to I-80 when traveling between the Mississippi River and Anamosa. Well-marked road signage will take you from Stone City through the villages of Wyoming, Monmouth, Baldwin, Maquoketa, Andrew, and Springbrook to finally arrive at Bellevue on the Mississippi. You can read more about the country drive and download a map online.

While driving along Iowa's byways, you'll see landscapes much like what Grant Wood saw, such as what he painted in View from Ellis Park, 1st Fairway *(1919).* 11 x 14 in., oil on board. Des Moines Art Center Permanent Collections; Gift of Betty R. Miorris, 1998.49. Photo: Ray Andrews

Starlighters II Community Theatre

136 E. Main St., Anamosa
319-462-4793
www.starlighters.org

Grant Wood was a passionate amateur thespian, so consider taking in some local performances. In operation since 1973, this award-winning nonprofit theater offers seasonal productions as well as acting classes.

Grant Wood Art Festival

Anamosa Library and Lawrence Park
600 E. Main St., Anamosa
319-521-4486 or 319-462-6181
www.anamosachamber.org/grant
woodartfestival

The Grant Wood Art Festival is held in a lovely park setting.   Anamosa Chamber of Commerce

This regional art festival, which has been held annually since 1972, commemorates the work of Wood and other Stone City Art Colony artists. The date of the one-day summer event varies, so check the current year's schedule of events on the website. A juried art show is displayed at the Anamosa Library, along with original work from the Stone City colony days. Each year the organizers like to feature a different retrospective solo exhibition of one Midwestern artist who participated in the art colony in the 1930s. Regional art is displayed and sold in the adjacent Lawrence Park. Live music and street performers entertain the crowd.

Daly Creek Winery

106 N. Ford St., Anamosa
319-462-2525
www.dalycreekwinery.com
Open 11-9 Tues.-Sat., 11-3 Sun.

This winery is operated by a local family who has farmed their land since 1854. They use the former creamery of the dairy for the current winery. Their sauvignon blanc is named Gothic White in honor of Grant Wood.

Study for Agricultural Science Mural *(1934), Grant Wood*
Oil on board, 32¾ x 47¾ in.. Museum purchase, Mrs. G. F. Van Vechten fund and Gift
of Peter M. Turner in memory of David Turner III. 90.7. Cedar Rapids Museum of Art

2 CEDAR RAPIDS
Artistic Evolution

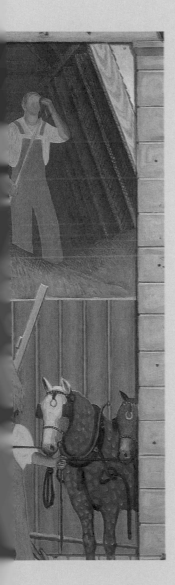

*I am willing to go so far as to say
that I believe the hope of a native
American art lies in the development of regional art centers and the
competition between them. It seems
the one way to the building up of an
honestly art-conscious America.*
—Grant Wood,
Revolt Against the City

Grant Wood divided his life into three parts
when he was interviewed by journalists: his
childhood; his "bohemian years" in the 1910s
and 1920s, when he attended art school, traveled to
Europe, and painted in the impressionist style; and his
Regionalist period after returning from Munich in
1929. Cedar Rapids was the locus for all three periods
in his life.

Cedar Rapids was part of the territory of the Fox
and Sac tribes before the first permanent white settler,
Osgood Shepherd, arrived in 1838. The town was first
named Columbus and later renamed Cedar Rapids
after the rapids in the Cedar River and the cedar trees
that adorned its banks. The city lies on both sides of the
Cedar River, 20 miles north of Iowa City and 100 miles
east of the state capital, Des Moines. When the Sinclair
Meat Factory was established in Cedar Rapids in 1871,
the city became more powerful. It remains one of the
most important cities in the world for corn processing.

In addition to Grant Wood, Cedar Rapids has been
home to many famous figures, including journalist and
historian William L. Shirer; writer and photographer

Carl Van Vechten; aerodynamics pioneer Dr. Alexander Lippisch; and actors Bobby Driscoll, Ashton Kutcher, and Elijah Wood. Rather surprisingly, it was also the home of Paul Tibbets, the pilot in command of the B-29 *Enola Gay* that dropped the atomic bomb on Hiroshima, adding to the heroic mystique of this small city with big figures in the iconography of the American psyche. The city is also the setting for the musical *The Pajama Game,* based on Richard Bissell's novel *7½ Cents.*

Cedar Rapids is nicknamed the City of Five Seasons, with the fifth season representing the time to enjoy the other four seasons. This seems very in keeping with the slightly self-reflective feeling of the city. The nickname is personified in the *Tree of Five Seasons* sculpture, which is downtown along the north side of the riverbank on First Avenue. You will see representations of the sculpture in many forms throughout the city.

Wood began his time in Cedar Rapids in 1901 at the age of 10, when his father died and his mother sold the Anamosa family farm. He attended Washington High School, where he later worked as a teacher and painted friezes in the same buildings in which he had studied. On the day he graduated from high school in 1910, he took a night train north to attend the Minneapolis School of Design. Over the next six years he took art classes there, as well as at the University of Iowa and the Art Institute of Chicago, but he always maintained his connection to Cedar Rapids.

When his mother fell on hard times in 1916, he returned to the city. He felt an obligation to provide a home for his sister and mother, as both of his brothers had married and moved away. After serving in World War I, he taught in the Cedar Rapids school system from 1919 to 1925. He built two homes for his family in the city, the first a rustic cottage that served as an interim home, and then 3178 Grove Court, where they lived from 1917 to 1925. In 1925 they moved to the Turner Mortuary carriage house at 5 Turner Alley and renovated the loft into a studio. In a conscious act of self-creation, there Wood fashioned theatrical curtains and performed plays, creating an artistic network of colleagues to enlarge his world to meet his spiritual and creative needs and feed his ambitious drive.

Cedar Rapids also provided a refuge and served as a place of personal rebirth for Wood after he returned from Paris in 1926. This trip can only be seen as a defeat after his solo exhibition received no adulation and was viewed as behind the times, as it included impressionistic landscapes during the height of cubist and post-cubist experimentation. As Winston Churchill believed, a man's measure of character and success is how he responds to his failures, and Wood responded by using Cedar Rapids as a base camp for his subsequent expeditions into his imagination. There he forged his own style and created paintings that would put him on world stage.

Thus it is not surprising that the Cedar Rapids Museum of Art houses a vast collection of Wood's work, as well as an impressive collection of other artists associated with him, including Marvin Cone, whose work can also be seen at the Stewart Library at Coe College, a few minutes' walk from the museum. In addition to those devoted to the museum and the college, the other attractions in this section will guide you to important places in Grant Wood's life in Cedar Rapids, expose you to the wide range of creative expression made by this native genius, and reveal the role Wood had in the community. By visiting the places he knew and painted, and seeing the context of his work and the achievements of his colleagues, his vision will become better understood.

Other cultural sites include the Paramount Theatre, the National Czech and Slovak Museum, the African American Historical Museum, and the Iowa Cultural Corridor Alliance. The city is also home to the National Muslim Cemetery, said to be the first exclusively Muslim cemetery in North America, and the Mother Mosque of America (ca. 1934), the longest standing mosque in North America. A Quaker Oats mill still dominates the north side of downtown and offers an interesting tour. City Hall and the county courthouse are located in the center of town, but on their own island, called Mays, on the Cedar River. (Cedar Rapids is one of few cities in the world with governmental offices on a municipal island.)

Today Cedar Rapids, population 128,000, is the second-largest city in the

War memorial on May Island   William Balthazar Rose

state of Iowa. It can be compared to a modern-day Florence, with blocks of wonderful commercial architecture that pay testament to the economic prosperity in Iowa after World War I. There is a sense of grandeur and excitement revealed in the wide range of architectural styles and urban configurations of the city, the art deco downtown buildings and small-scale skyscrapers reminiscent of a film set for the *Superman* television series of the 1940s. A drive through the city reveals a dynamic tableau: A range of grain silos, skyscrapers, bridges, and raised freeways make the experience poignant

The small island within the Cedar River calls to mind the Île de la Cité on the Seine in Paris. City of Cedar Rapids

and memorable. The fact that it is a city repetitiously subjected to floods and economic recessions only adds to the sense of heroism that pervades it. The government center on its small island within the Cedar River calls to mind the Île de la Cité on the Seine in Paris, but the mom-and-pop restaurants, museums, and architectural curiosities establish it as a Midwestern gem.

For more information on the area, contact the Cedar Rapids Area Convention & Visitors Bureau, 119 First Avenue SE, Cedar Rapids; 800-735-5557; www.cedar-rapids.com.

CEDAR RAPIDS MUSEUM OF ART

410 Third Ave. SE, Cedar Rapids
319-366-7503
www.crma.org
Open noon–4 Tues., Wed., Fri., and Sun.; noon–8 Thurs.;
and 10–4 Sat.; closed Mon. and major holidays
Admission: $5 adults, $4 seniors and students, and free for children under 18; free for all visitors 4–8 Thurs.

It was **Grant Wood's dream** that Cedar Rapids should have a museum, and the current museum exists in part due to his efforts, representing his dedication to forging an art center in the city. The Cedar Rapids Museum of Art (CRMA) was originally an art club formed in 1895, later becoming the Cedar Rapids Art Association, with a gallery in the Carnegie Library. Today it has

Cedar Rapids Museum of Art, west entrance   City of Cedar Rapids

the largest collection of Grant Wood paintings in the world. In 1989 the museum opened the now famous addition designed by the splashy architect Charles W. Moore, known for his Piazza d'Italia (New Orleans) and Kresge College (University of California, Santa Cruz). In 2002 the museum acquired the Grant Wood Studio (see page 27), and it has important collections of Marvin Cone and other contemporary Iowan artists. In addition to Wood's paintings, the museum exhibits the cartoons he made for the stained-glass memorial window in the Veterans Memorial Building (see the "Veterans Memorial Building Stained-Glass Window" attraction). These drawings are truly amazing; they are life-size, the principal one being exhibited horizontally on the floor. Other works from the collections of Grant Wood and Marvin Cone that are not on display may be viewed by appointment. The curatorial staff is extremely friendly and helpful.

As you walk around the museum, be sure not to miss the following pieces.

Woman with Plants (1929), Grant Wood

This is a portrait of Grant Wood's mother, Hattie, and could be compared to the famous portrait painted by James Whistler of his own mother. It is interesting that both painters made such profound images of their female parents—undoubtedly they both had intense connections to their mothers. In Wood's case his relationship with his mother was particularly strong after he lost his aloof father at age 10. This work, which is among the most labored paintings made by Wood, is also in his "new" style, which he adopted after he returned from Europe for the last time. His new style was influenced by the Flemish northern school, in particular painters like Hans Holbein and Hans Memling, a style that expresses the search for deeper roots than the impressionism he had until that time emulated.

Wood attempted to paint a vision of his mother waiting for him upon his return from overseas; it is symbolic, and important, as he would not return to Europe again. That chapter was closed for good. The plant held by his mother is symbolic of what was to come—the flowering of his career with a new and more determined style and public acclaim. In Paris Wood had

Woman with Plants (*1929*), *Grant Wood*
Oil on upsom board, 20½ x 17⅞ in., Museum purchase. 31.1. Cedar Rapids Museum of Art

received almost no attention; however, this painting shortly precedes *American Gothic* and international fame. As a portrait it is imbued with tenderness and severity. The mother's faraway look suggests loss, and there is an almost mystical inclination to her gaze and posture, with her hands holding the cylindrical flower pot near her womb, and her eyes, while looking off into the distance, hinting at unknowable thoughts.

Mourner's Bench (ca. 1921–1922), Grant Wood

The *Mourner's Bench* is a hilarious piece typical of Wood's irreverent humor, multiplied by all the innuendos and homoerotic content one could infer if one wished when studying the carved wooden seat. The inscription carved deep into the bench's back reads, THE WAY OF THE TRANSGRESSOR IS HARD, namely, as hard as the oak of the bench seat and at least as splintery. Adorning the bench are three very humorous faces, shrieking with the rapturous enjoyment of minor transgressors. A school bench made for bad boys, it was, in fact, constructed by schoolboys under Grant's supervision, and it stood outside the high school principal's office in Cedar Rapids.

This wonderful, unique bench in part expresses Wood's devotion to Regionalism at the level of craft and construction, exemplifying his concern for

Mourner's Bench (*ca. 1921–1922*), *Grant Wood* Cedar Rapids Community School
District

the local manufacture of things. In this sense he was aligned with the teach-
ings of British designer William Morris (of which he was aware) and their per-
mutations in American Arts and Crafts. Wood seems to have had a wide and
experimental appetite as a creator. Not merely an easel painter, he involved
himself with jewelry, furniture, ironwork, and odd bits of sculpture, such as
the potted metal flowers also on display in this museum (*Lilies of the Alley*).

Agriculture: When Tillage Begins (1934), Grant Wood

This oil study for the murals in the library of Iowa State (see the "Parks Library" attraction in part 4) is a complete and edifying example of how Wood
was able to very clearly envision a mural of almost more than life-size propor-
tions. Everything about the mural—from the colors to the placement of figures
and the architectural backdrop of the barn—has been defined; it is almost as
if it was painted after the fact, it is so clearly resolved. The study suggests just
how literal the process of painting murals was for Wood, and how he used
traditional methods of enlargement, such as scaling from a grid, to create a
massive mural. In this sense he resembles an architect, with this study representing a working drawing for the mural. Wood became the director of the
Public Works of Art Project (PWAP) for the state of Iowa under the Works
Progress Administration (WPA) and was responsible for administrating a large
number of murals in the state.

Adoration of the Home *(1921–1922), Grant Wood*
Oil on canvas attached to a wood panel, 22¾ x 81⅜ in.
Gift of Mr. and Mrs. Peter F Bezanson. 80.1. Cedar Rapids Museum of Art

Adoration of the Home (1921–1922), Grant Wood

This painting was commissioned by local real estate agent Henry Ely, who said of Wood that he "never bartered his birthright for a one-way ticket to any hot bed of culture." It is an unabashed celebration of small-town prosperity and, in particular, Cedar Rapids. Though in some ways this work of Wood's is one of the most difficult to come to grips with, and it is most criticized as having unfortunate similarities with realist political art of less-than-appetizing regimes of the same historical period, it is also arguably an advancement of decent democratic and American values that are quite palatable and human.

In all fairness, the painting is espousing Wood's vision of democracy, a vision located in a regional sensibility: small-town, slightly awkward, knowable, agrarian, and industrial, with protagonists like one's uncle and childhood friends who act as participants in a world that is almost Jeffersonian. It expresses the values in which city and country are brought together in idealized harmony. Men and women unite to celebrate the construction of a humble wooden house, and yet the painting operates in a sort of monumental and realistic classicism.

Although the world Wood portrays seems a long distance from Stalinist works from the same era, the type of representation is essentially similar, and this sense of academic detachment is perhaps a little alarming. The painting raises the problem of all political art that is used to substantiate a regime: The oversimplified and idealized figures begin to appear slightly unreal and interchangeable, perhaps becoming hard and soulless tools for the advancement of the political machine. What saves Wood here is that the political machine is small-scale, agrarian, and regional. If there is corruption, it is small-town corruption—not the depravity of an overpoliticized state.

This painting is important in that it is an example of Wood's attempt to give voice to the political and to come to grips with that aspect of personification. Wood seemed to rarely involve himself with religious painting but rather with historical, political, and national issues, which reverberate in much of his work to some extent.

Portrait of John B. Turner (1928–1930), Grant Wood

The sitter for this work was the father of David Turner, one of Wood's best patrons, who provided him with a studio next to his mortuary business (see "Turner Mortuary"). John Turner described this painting as a portrait of "two old maps," in reference to the 1869 map of Linn County seen behind the sitter. The painting, which has been dated twice (in 1928 and 1930), is in fact a rectangular painting originally placed in an oval frame.

Wood attempted to give a pictorial voice to the Midwestern character, and this painting, along with *American Gothic* and *Woman with Plants,* most fully realize this intention. The sitter scrutinizes and is scrutinized; the overall effect is dull, terrifying, and unfriendly, academic yet mesmerizing. Wood evokes history and creates the pioneer in a painting that seemingly exudes dust.

Cartoons for the Veterans Memorial Window (1927–1929), Grant Wood

These life-size drawings on brown paper are not to be missed. The largest, measuring more than 24 by 20 feet, is a complete working drawing displayed on the floor. Wood made these as preparatory studies for the stained-glass window in the Veterans Memorial Building on the municipal island in Cedar Rapids (see "Veterans Memorial Building Stained-Glass Window").

Wood made these drawings in Cedar Rapids and then brought them to Munich, Germany, where they were used as the basis for the creation and construction of the window, which remains as testimony of Grant Wood's skill in design. In the drawings he envisages in great detail the figures of the final piece, including each piece of glass, while simultaneously resolving issues of structure and overall harmony. A Renaissance man with a wide creative range, Wood also designed camouflage for the army; look closely for such patterns that he couldn't resist adding to the stained glass!

Lilies of the Alley
(ca. 1925), Grant Wood

These expressive sculptures, made of wire, plaster, bottle tops, paint, and ceramics, have a toylike feeling, demonstrating a playful aspect of Wood's

Lilies of the Alley (*ca. 1925*), *Grant Wood* Found objects (clothespin) and earthenware pot, 12 x 12x 6½ in. Gift of Harriet Y. and John B Turner II. 72.12.38. Cedar Rapids Museum of Art nature. Almost reminiscent of beatnik art of the 1950s, with their slightly funky construction, junky materials, and crude forms, they reveal a side of Wood that could experiment endlessly and was not afraid of low art (rather than the realm of high art he tended to explore). Wood often gave these objects away as gifts.

Old Shoes
(1926), Grant Wood

This small work is typical of Wood's early phase as a painter, which can be loosely described as impressionistic largely due to his several trips to Paris, where he absorbed the lessons of the impressionists. His work of this period was looser in style and quite experimental, accommodating the various traits of other artists as far-reaching as Bonnard and Monet, the Englishman Sickert, Van Gogh, and so on. It can be fairly said that he had not yet found his own style, and it was necessary for him to jettison this type of painting before he could reveal his more profound works. The motif of shoes is one most powerfully expressed by Van Gogh, and this painting recalls the boots painted by him. These are, however, the dress shoes of a playboy or banker or merchant, while Van Gogh's were the boots of a common laborer.

Old Shoes *(1926), Grant Wood* Oil on composition board, 10 x 10 in. Gift of Harriet Y. and John B. Turner II. 76.2.3. Cedar Rapids Museum of Art

Seed Time and Harvest
(1937), Grant Wood

In the late 1930s and early 1940s, Wood made several lithographs that were sold through the Associated American Artists, a mail-order firm based in New York. This is one of several lithographs Wood made illustrating the seasons and rural events. His work in lithography demonstrates just how versatile he could be and his capacity to turn his hand to almost any medium.

Seed Time and Harvest *(1937), Grant Wood* Lithograph on paper, 7⅜ x 12⅛ in. Gift of Mr. Peter O. Stamats and Mr. Larry K. Zirbel. 85.6.2. Cedar Rapids Museum of Art

Portrait of Grant Wood (ca. 1935), Christian Petersen

This expressive sculpture conveys all of Wood's humor and pathos, and to a large extent also his heavyset, almost clumsy physique. It was created by Wood's long-term associate Christian Petersen, who worked with him at Iowa State University (see part 4).

GRANT WOOD STUDIO AND HOME

810 Second Ave. SE, Cedar Rapids
319-366-7503

Open noon–4 Sat. and Sun. and by appointment; closed during winter
Admission: free

Grant Wood Studio and Home, Cedar Rapids   William Balthazar Rose

Lifetime patrons John B. Turner and his mortician son, David, offered Grant Wood rent-free use of the brick stable behind their funeral home. Grant Wood liked the studio space so much that he redecorated it and ingenuously outfitted it so that he could live there full time, moving from his home in Kenwood Park to the studio with his mother and sister, Nan. They lived there from 1924 to 1935. His retrofits included furniture designed to fit away into the dormers when not in use, and his amendments were so inventive that there was room in the hayloft for not only three adults and an art studio, but also for a theater for his amateur productions with his friends. A theater curtain he designed remains hanging in his studio today. Other clever improvements include beds that slip under cupboards; a bathtub that lowers into the floor so that there is enough room to stand in the low-ceiled bathroom; cupboard doors upholstered with the pockets of old blue jeans stiffened with plaster to hold utensils; and a front door with a glass panel painted to look like a clock, with hands that could be moved to point to the occupants' hour of return or current activity: OUT ON TOWN, TAKING A BATH, HAVING A PARTY, etc. The studio provided a mini kitchen, bathroom, and a bedroom for Ma Wood, and a large open space where Wood painted, entertained, ate, and slept. He and his sister, Nan,

Interior view of 5 Turner Alley, looking east, ca. 1925   Cedar Rapids Museum of Art Archives. Photo: John W. Barry

ABOVE: **Bibbed Overalls Cuboard Door** (*front*), *ca. 1925. A cupboard door plastered with bibbed overalls was one of the many ingenious touches Grant Wood made to his home.* Mixed media, 56 x 52¼. Gift of Harriet Y. and John B Turner II. 72.12.51. Cedar Rapids Museum of Art

RIGHT: **Door to 5 Turner Alley** (*1924*), **Grant Wood** Painted wood, fabric, glass, and wrought-iron, 78 x 29⅞ x 1¼ in. Gift of Harriet Y. and John B Turner II. 72.12.15. Cedar Rapids Museum of Art

slept in full proximity to the heavy fumes of his oil paint.

Wood and David Turner hoped to refurbish the other dilapidated buildings in the alley to mimic the studio, with the aim of attracting other artists to form a bohemian colony, but the structures would have been too costly to restore due to the economic pressures of the Depression. Wood was a driving force in local artistic circles, and he had hoped to create a Latin Quarter or Greenwich Village of eastern Iowa. He was active in art groups such as the Garlic Club—named after the French method of preparing a salad bowl by wiping it with garlic—created as an alternative to Shriner or Mason clubs.

The style of the studio was entirely Grant's own, though it was influenced by the Arts and Crafts movement. There are all kinds of details indicating the quirky character of the painter, and the crudeness of the design vaguely suggests a European peasant's home while also feeling a little bit Hollywood. Largely unaltered, the present studio museum is a great opportunity to see Wood's environs and understand the circumstances of his life. In its own way it is comparable to the studio and museum of Cézanne in Aix-en-Provence, France, and the re-created studio in the Morandi Museum in Bologna, Italy, though it reveals decidedly American ideas and sensibilities. It was here that Wood painted some of his most enduring paintings, including *American Gothic, Woman with Plants, Midnight Ride of Paul Revere,* and *Daughters of the Revolution.*

An excellent tour of the studio is available upon request, as well as a video on the life and times of Grant Wood. You can ask all the questions you want of the guide. The Armstrong Visitor Center, on the ground floor beneath the studio, has a gift shop and other amenities.

Wood poses next to his painting Arbor Day *in his studio, 1932, wearing his signature overalls and white shirt.*
Cedar Rapids Museum of Art. Photo: John W. Barry. 89.2.3

TURNER MORTUARY
810 Second Avenue SE, Cedar Rapids

Next to the Grant Wood Studio is the home that was owned by the Turner family. Wood created the design for the wrought-iron gate on the property, which he conceived to go along with the Colonial style of the house, though the actual design is more inventive and original than one would expect. He also designed the stained-glass windows on the side of the home adjacent to the studio. This type of work wasn't beyond the norm for Wood; like many artists, he needed additional income to fund his painting. Some of these jobs included interior design, window display work, and decorative art commissions such as the gate and window of the Turner home and the stained-glass window in Veterans Memorial Building (see next section).

This 1927 Christmas card created by Wood is a playful cross section showing him at work in his studio in the mortuary carriage house. Turner Alley Christmas Card, 1927, relief print with hand coloring, pen and ink, 10 x 7¼ in. Gift of John B. Turner II. 81.17.4. Cedar Rapids Museum of Art

Iron gates designed by Grant Wood at the Turner home William Balthazar Rose

The Turners were longtime patrons of Wood's, and so was the Palmer family, of Palmer Handwriting Method fame, which was widely used in schools for decades. A portrait of John B. Turner is on display at the Cedar Rapids Art Museum. The Turner home is now a privately owned funeral home.

VETERANS MEMORIAL STAINED-GLASS WINDOW

Veterans Memorial Building　　*319-286-5038*
50 Second Ave. Bridge,
Cedar Rapids

In his application for the commission for this window, Grant Wood reminded the decision makers that he was "both a Legionnaire and a local man" and that he was certain "no outside man could put into the window the work and devotion" that he would commit to it. Wood received the commission without any other bids being sought.

Some art historians insist that Wood saw and was influenced by the progressive German art movement Neue Sachlichkeit, or New Objectivity, when he was in Munich, where he had brought his design so it could be fabricated in stained glass. But it was not Wood's habit to study contemporary art. Wood

ABOVE: *Veterans Memorial Building*
William Balthazar Rose

LEFT: *Veterans Memorial Stained-Glass Window*
courtesy of Cedar Rapids Museum of Art

was later criticized as being unpatriotic for traveling to Germany to have the window made.

The study drawings for the window are on display at the Cedar Rapids Museum of Art, and in them, as in the window here, figures in uniform from each of the major wars fought by American soldiers are illustrated. Above them is the towering figure of a woman, presumably representing the republic. The work is a powerful and adventurous piece, and it signals Wood's continued interest in the Arts and Crafts movement.

The window is large and dramatic, but it's little known outside of Iowa, and the building has been closed due to damage sustained in the flooding of the Mississippi River in 2008. It is currently undergoing a $300,000 restoration. The Veterans Memorial Building is on Mays Island, a small island in the center of town, unusual if not unique in the United States.

Cedar Rapids River view of city
City of Cedar Rapids

The Old J. G. Cherry Plant (J. G. Cherry series, 1925), *Grant Wood*
Oil on composition board, 13¼ x 41¼ in. On permanent loan from the Cherry Burrell Charitable
Foundation 74.5.4. Cedar Rapids Museum of Art

 ## J. G. CHERRY PLANT

The Ceramics Center   *www.theceramicscenter.org*
319 10th Ave. SE, Suite 117,   *Open 3–9 Mon., 9–9 Tues.–Thurs.,*
Cedar Rapids   *9–4 Fri., and 10–4 Sat.*
319-365-9644

You can see the dairy equipment manufacturing factory that was the subject of a series of paintings by Grant Wood, including *The Old J. G. Cherry
Plant* (1925), which are housed at
the Cedar Rapids Museum of Art.
The series depicts the exterior of the
Victorian brick factory building as
well as scenes of workmen from the
factory employed in different tasks,
glorifying the nobility of the common
man and the technologies of the day.
The series, which is reminiscent of
Van Gogh's studies of weavers in
Holland, was commissioned by the
owner of the factory, J. G. Cherry.
Cherry's choice of Wood for the
commission makes sense. Wood was
employed by the University of Iowa
and Iowa State University both as an
instructor and as a fine artist to cre-

The Coil Welder (J. G. Cherry series,
1925), *Grant Wood*
Oil on canvas, 18⅛ x 22 in. On permanent loan
from the Cherry Burrell Charitable Foundation
74.5.2. Cedar Rapids Museum of Art

ABOVE: *The old Cherry plant is now used as an artists' cooperative.*
William Balthazar Rose

RIGHT: The Shop Inspector (J. G. Cherry series, 1925), *Grant Wood*
Oil on canvas, 24 x 18⅛ in. On permanent loan from the Cherry Burrell Charitable Foundation 74.5.6. Cedar Rapids Museum of Art

ate murals, and land grant universities at the time, and still today, position themselves as proponents of scientific approaches to farming and innovators in industrialized food production.

Today the old factory building is the home of the Ceramics Center, cooperative studio space and a sales outlet for more than 40 artists, including painters, metal workers, glass blowers, sculptors, and ceramicists. You are welcome to go inside to meet the artists and shop. The center's biggest retail event is the Very Cherry Holiday Sale, held the first Saturday of December.

CEDAR RAPIDS SCHOOLS

2205 Forest Dr. SE,   319-558-2000
Cedar Rapids   www.cr.k12.ia.us

The Cedar Rapids School District, where Grant Wood studied and later taught, has an extensive collection of his art on display. You will need to call each building for an appointment and permission to visit. The schools also have artwork by Marvin Cone, a friend of Wood's who went to high school with him in Cedar Rapids.

Washington High School (2205 Forest Dr. SE, Cedar Rapids; 319-558-4350). Here you can see the friezes that Grant Wood painted with his

ABOVE: *Grant Wood and his McKinley Junior High School art students working on* Imagination Iles Frieze, *1924.* Cedar Rapids Museum of Art Archive

RIGHT: **Indian Creek** (*1929*), *Grant Wood* Oil on canvas. 22 x 17¾ in. Museum purchase, Save-the-Art Fund with gift of Elliot-Green and others. 2007.039b Cedar Rapids Museum of Art

students' assistance, as well as several oil paintings donated by Wood to the school.

   McKinley Elementary (620 10th St. SE, Cedar Rapids; 319-558-2348). This school has a frieze, a school play backdrop, lithographs, and a papier-mâché mask.

   Grant Wood Elementary (645 26th St. SE, Cedar Rapids; 319-558-2467). The school has several drawings by Wood.

   Franklin Middle School (2205 Forest Dr. SE, Cedar Rapids; 319-558-2452). The middle school has a wonderful Wood painting called *Indian Creek*.

 COE COLLEGE, STEWART MEMORIAL LIBRARY

1220 First Ave. NE,   *www.coe.edu*
Cedar Rapids   *Open 11–1 Sun.–Thurs.,*
319-399-8585 or   *9–6 Fri. and Sat.*
319-366-7503   *Admission: free*

Charming Coe College is a short distance from the Cedar Rapids Museum of Art and the Grant Wood Studio. The college's impressive Stewart Memorial Library hosts four galleries, two of which are dedicated to Grant

Pink Silo (1961), *Marvin Cone*   George T. Henry College Archives, Stewart Memorial Library, Coe College

Wood's friend Marvin Cone, who graduated from the college as well as taught art there for four decades. If you've seen the collection of Cone's work in the Cedar Rapids Museum of Art, it may have whet your appetite for more, and there's quite a bit more to see here: The Stewart Memorial Library has at least 60 works spanning his entire career. For Marvin Cone enthusiasts, this is the place to best appreciate his work.

In addition to the two gallery spaces dedicated to Cone's work, the library has other galleries, including the Reva and John Pashgian Gallery and the Conger Metcalf Gallery. The latter is dedicated to 1936 Coe graduate Conger Metcalf, who studied with Wood and Cone at the Stone City Art Colony and went on to become well-known in the Boston art community. Important to the study of Grant Wood is the Knapp study room, which hosts 15 photographs by Iowa photographer John W. Barry, who also studied at the Stone City Art Colony. The Perrine Gallery, on the second floor, displays 12 of the 14 works by Wood that the university owns. *The Fruits of Iowa,* as the series is known, was originally commissioned for a coffee shop in the Montrose Hotel in Cedar Rapids. These murals,

Uncle Ben's Door (1958), *Marvin Cone*   32 x 16 in., 1958, oil on canvas. Des Moines Art Center Permanent Collections; Susan Ankeny Brown Memorial Fund, 1958.28. Photo: Rich Sanders

painted in oil on canvas, represent Wood at his most bucolic and sentimental. Supporting these paintings are several minor works by Wood, including an important study for *Daughters of the Revolution.*

Art Insight: Marvin Cone

Marvin Dorwart Cone was born in Cedar Rapids in 1891. In 1906 he met Grant Wood while they were both students at Washington High School in Cedar Rapids, which began a lifelong friendship. They both contributed drawings to the high school yearbook, designed theater sets, and participated in the Cedar Rapids Art Association. After graduation, he attended Coe College, and then studied at the Art Institute of Chicago for two years.

Like Wood, Cone served during World War I, enlisting in the Iowa National Guard's 34th Infantry Division in 1917. During basic training, he won a design competition for his Red Bull insignia, which the unit wears to this day. He served in France as an interpreter for two years, after which he studied at the Ecole des Beaux Arts in Montpellier. When he returned to Cedar Rapids in 1919, he continued to pursue his interest in art. He considered commercial art but chose instead to accept a position teaching French at Coe College. Cone renewed his friendship with Grant Wood upon his return, resuming his involvement with the local art association (now the Cedar Rapids Museum of Art). In 1919 Killian's Department Store hosted a joint

exhibition of the two artists' work in Cedar Rapids.

In the summer of 1920, when they were both 29, Cone and Wood traveled to Paris together in the hopes of improving their technical skills. The visit proved influential, resulting in a stunning series of impressionistic views of picturesque cityscapes and landscapes, Parisian streets and gardens, and the French countryside by both artists. Wood returned to Paris alone in 1923 and again in 1926, after

Marvin Cone in Paris, 1920. Photo taken by Grant Wood. Silver print on paper, 11 x 14 in. Cedar Rapids Museum of art archive. S7.8. Courtesy of Cedar Rapids Museum of Art

Dotted about in the library display areas is a good collection of American and European art, including works by such renowned artists as Graham Sutherland, Henri Matisse, Pablo Picasso, Andy Warhol, Leonard Baskin, and Aristide Maillol. There are also less well-known ones who are nevertheless well worth appreciating, including Thomas Nast, Benjamin Kopman, and Raymond Guerrier.

The library galleries are something of an unexpected revelation, where

River Bend
No 5 (1938),
Marvin Cone
Oil on canvas,
24 x 30⅛ in.
Gift of Isobel
Howell Brown.
81.1. Cedar Rapids
Museum of Art

which he arranged his first commercial gallery show, an unsuccessful exhibition of 47 paintings at the Galerie Carmine. After Wood returned to the United States for the last time, Cone helped him found the Stone City Art Colony east of Cedar Rapids in 1932.

Cone lived all his life in Cedar Rapids, where he married, raised a family, and taught art at Coe College for more than four decades. Although he never achieved great fame, he was highly respected by his contemporaries. Many of his paintings can be seen in Cedar Rapids, and some of his work is in the permanent collection of the University of Northern Iowa's

Gallery of Art in Cedar Falls and the Blanden Memorial Art Museum in Fort Dodge. He died in 1965 at the age of 74, and his widow, Winnifred, donated many of his paintings to Coe College, where they are displayed in the library.

Landscape fascinated Cone, and he sought to evoke his inner vision of nature rather than to create a realistic depiction of it. To Cone, nature was a vehicle for revealing certain truths. He once said, "The purpose of art is not to reproduce life, but to present an editorial, a comment on life.... The artist does not set out to imitate nature. What would be the purpose of that?"

one can see two major collections of unlauded but significant American painters of the first half of the 20th century. Cone and Metcalf provide a fascinating insight into the American psyche and the issues facing painters in provincial America. It must also be stressed that both Cone and Metcalf are painters who knew Wood's work well and worked alongside him on some of his most illustrious projects.

While you are here, be sure to appreciate the following pieces.

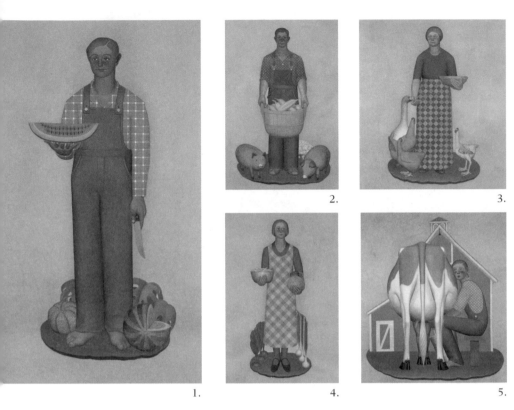

1. Farmer's Son with Watermelon *(1932), Grant Wood*
2. Farmer with Pigs and Corn, *Grant Wood, from the 1932 Fruits of Iowa series*
3. Farmer's Wife with Chickens, *Grant Wood, from the 1932 Fruits of Iowa series*
4. Farmer's Daughter with Vegetables, *Grant Wood, from the 1932 Fruits of Iowa series*
5. Boy Milking Cow, Grant Wood, *from the 1932 Fruits of Iowa series*

George T. Henry College Archives, Stewart Memorial Library, Coe College

Malnutrition (1919), Grant Wood

This somewhat harrowing portrait of Cone reveals all the depth of understanding and empathetic turmoil Wood felt for his friend. It almost recalls the paintings of the Scandinavian painter Edvard Munch.

Farmer's Son with Watermelon (1932), Grant Wood

Part of *The Fruits of Iowa* series, commissioned for a coffee shop in a fancy downtown hotel, this work demonstrates Wood at his most sentimental. There is a peachy glow to the painting, and everything is presented in almost a streamlined softness. It is perhaps most reminiscent of Norman Rockwell in its suggestion of American values and nostalgic yearning for an idealized agrarian identity.

Study for *Daughters of the Revolution* (1932), Grant Wood

This drawing, a study for Wood's painting *Daughters of the Revolution,* reveals the deft hand of a master draftsman, and it communicates succinctly Wood's ability to confirm a clear idea for a painting in a preliminary way. The painting *Daughters of the Revolution,* on display at the Cincinnati Art Museum, is powerful in its irony and bitterness, comparing the heroics of George Washington and his revolutionaries with the critical petty faces of Iowan women having tea at an elite society meeting.

Grant Wood poses next to his painting Daughters of the Revolution *at 5 Turner Alley, 1932* Courtesy of Cedar Rapids Museum of Art Archives

Shadowed Door No. 2 (1961), Marvin Cone

This is something of a culminating work and shows Cone at his most enigmatic and mysterious. The layering of influences is compelling; the tone of the painting appears solitary and haunting. It is as if the artist transmuted the metaphysical paintings of the Italian artist de Chirico through the eyes of American ruralism, yielding a work so mesmerizing that it recalls the isolated tensions of Andrew Wyeth.

Thunderhead No. 3 (1942–1943), Marvin Cone

Cone seems to have created two types of signature paintings. One is the mysterious geometric interiors of doorways, as seen in *Three Doorways, Shadowed Door No. 2,* and *Shadowed Door No. 3,* and the other is typified by this painting of clouds, in which colors are heightened and the sky predominates over the land. These works are truly original and yet seem to be unknown outside the state of Iowa. Another painting to seek out at the library is *Clouds.*

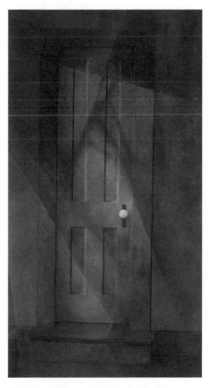

Shadowed Door No.2 *(1961),* Marvin Cone George T. Henry College Archives, Stewart Memorial Library, Coe College

Thunderhead No. 3
(*1942–1943*),
Marvin Cone
George T. Henry College
Archives, Stewart Memorial
Library, Coe College

The Big Top (1936), Marvin Cone

Cone was captivated by circuses and painted innumerable versions of them. Circus performers, like artists, struggle to entertain through feats of daring and skill, but they do not have a solid justification for their trade as they provide nothing practical. Members of both professions also were accustomed to the poverty that usually came with their trades. Cone was fortunate to become a tenured teacher at Coe College, a secure position without something comparable in the world of the circus performer.

TODAY'S LANDSCAPE
Ancillary Art and Ecoattractions

Grant Wood Nature Trail

Linn County Trails Association
P.O. Box 2681, Cedar Rapids, IA 52406
http://linncountytrails.org/maps/find-a-trail/grant-wood-trail/

The Grant Wood Nature trail, an 8.5-mile paved walking and biking trail that includes Linn and Jones Counties, travels from Marion east toward Mount Vernon. Along the way visitors will enjoy native prairie flowers and typical Iowa farms with their rolling landscape. The tidy fenced farm fields are reminiscent of the tamed squares of prairie that Grant Wood drapes in his landscapes like one of his mother's quilts.

Downtown Farmer's Market

Downtown Cedar Rapids
www.downtowncr.org/Content/Farmers-Market.aspx

The Downtown Farmer's Market is by far the largest in the area, featuring more than 200 vendors and entertainment. Check the website for the hours, which vary seasonally. There are also other farmer's markets in the area; for more information, check http://thegazette.com/farmersmarkets/.

Quaker Oats Factory Tour

418 Second St. NE, Cedar Rapids
319-362-3121
Tours for small groups by appointment
Admission: free

After the Cedar River was dammed in 1844, the first mill in Cedar Rapids was constructed, and the city began its role as one of America's most important food-processing centers. By the turn of the 20th century, the Stuart family had founded North Star Oatmeal Milling, which today is operated as Quaker Oats. The tour shows various rooms of the factory dedicated to oat processing and sorting. Be a sleuth and match the aroma with the product of the day's production run.

National Czech and Slovak Cultural Museum

1400 Inspiration Pl. SW, Cedar Rapids
319-362-8500
www.ncsml.org
Open 10–5 Mon.–Sat., noon–4 Sun; closed Thanksgiving,
Christmas, and New Year's Day
Admission: $12 adults, $10 seniors, $5 students and military,
$3 children 6–12, free for children 5 and under

During Grant Wood's time, many of the citizens of Cedar Rapids could trace their roots to eastern Europe. (Wood himself was British, with Pennsylvania Quaker roots on his father's side and New England Puritan roots on his mother's.) The original museum on 16th Avenue was destroyed due to damage from the Mississippi River flood of 2008, and it was reopened at this new location in 2012.

Brucemore

2160 Linden Dr. SE, Cedar Rapids
319-362-7375
www.brucemore.org

A National Trust Historic Site, Brucemore mansion was the home of several families, but it focuses on the time the Douglas family inhabited the mansion, from 1915 to 1925. In addition to discussing the families who lived in the home, guides explore such themes as the experiences of servants, technology, arts and music, and life on a country estate.

Brucemore hosts numerous events throughout the year, including a garden show, holiday open houses, children's activities, garden walks, concerts, lectures, workshops, and educational programs. The Bluesmore blues festival held on the First Avenue lawn attracts thousands, and Brucemore's outdoor natural amphitheater stages a range of productions—from Greek tragedy and Shakespearean comedy to 20th-century American drama—during the summer.

Attendees bring lawn chairs and picnic baskets for a magical evening with a lush backdrop incorporated into the action—actors emerge from the woods, get dunked in the pond near the theater, and help themselves to the audience's picnics. Advance tickets are $15–30. For details about the outdoor productions, call 319-398-0449 or visit www.cedar-rapids.com/partners/play/theater-performing-arts.

Art Galleries

Local artists are showcased at two small art galleries: the **Campbell Steele Gallery** (1064 Seventh Ave., Marion; 319-373-9211; www.campbellsteele .com) and **ARA Gallery and Interiors** (4850 Armar Dr. SE, Cedar Rapids; Tony Alt: 319-366-2520; www.aragallery.net). Visit their websites to learn about current exhibitions and hours.

SPT Theatre Company

115 Third St. SE, Cedar Rapids
319-361-5297
www.spttheatre.org

SPT was founded in 2006 as a small professional community theater to expand performing opportunities for artists. Productions include serious drama and writer's readings. To find out the current season's repertoire, visit the theater's website.

Pleasant Creek State Park

County Road W36, Palo
319-436-7716
www.iowadnr.gov/Destinations/StateParksRecAreas.aspx
Open daily during daylight hours
Admission: free

If you are up for a longer expedition, locals recommend the trails at Pleasant Creek. You can download maps at the Linn County Trails Association's website, http://linncountytrails.org.

Morgan Creek Park

7515 Worchester Rd., Palo
319-892-6450
http://linncountytrails.org
Open daily during daylight hours
Admission: free

Morgan Creek is a quiet county park where you can have a picnic and appreciate the majestic clouds that meander across the prairie sky like ghosts of bison. See if you can transport yourself into a Cone or Wood landscape here during your exploration. Downloadable maps are available at the Linn County Trails Association website, http://linncountytrails.org.

Linn County Fair
201 Central City Rd., Central City
319-929-3247
http://thelinncountyfair.com

The Linn County Fair is held annually during the summer in advance of the Iowa State Fair, so that county winners can advance to the state competition. Not much will have changed since Grant Wood attended: See everything from crafts and artwork to horse races and livestock judging. Summer dates vary year to year, so visitors will need to visit the website to see the current year's schedule. However, if the timing does not coincide with your summertime visit to Iowa, consider doing an Internet search for other county fairs—there are 99 counties in Iowa, so there are lots of options.

Cedar Ridge Vineyards
501 Seventh Ave. SE, Cedar Rapids
319-362-2778
www.crwine.com
Open 11–9 Wed.–Fri., 11–5 Sat., and 11–6 Sun.

Cedar Ridge Vineyards winery and distillery creates 10 wines, varying from a sweet white to a dry red. It is the only licensed distillery in Iowa, creating Clearheart vodka, grappa, and apple brandy.

Annual Art Festivals

There are several art festivals held in this area each year. The dates vary from year to year, so be sure to check the websites.

Marion Arts Festival (1225 Sixth Ave., Suite 100, Marion; 319-377-6316; www.marionartsfestival.com). Consistently named among the top tier of juried art events nationwide, the Marion Arts Festival presents 50 artists offering fine arts and crafts to an audience of 16,000. Hosted at the City Square Park.

Legion Art Festival (1103 Third St. SE, Cedar Rapids; 319-364-1580; http://legionarts.org). This not-for-profit organization showcases contemporary art during this festival, based in the 1891 CSPS Hall on the edge of Cedar Rapids. The organization also presents cutting-edge film, theater, and art in a variety of venues.

Eco-Arts Fest (Czech Village New Bohemia Main Street District, 101 16th Ave. SW, Suite A, Cedar Rapids; 319-432-9785; http://newboczech.info /eco-arts-fest). The event varies year to year; please "Czech" the website for the current year's offerings.

Young Corn *(1931), Grant Wood*

Oil on masonite panel, 24 x 29⅞ in. Collection of the Cedar Rapids
Community School District, on loan to Cedar Rapids Museum of Art.

3 SOUTHEAST IOWA

Life Struggles and the Search for Self

> The main thing is to teach students
> to think, and if they can—to Feel
> —GRANT WOOD,
> REVOLT AGAINST THE CITY

I owa City is a tragic chapter in Grant Wood's life. In what would have been expected to be a positive culmination of his mature life, his marriage and his academic post at the University of Iowa were instead fraught with disappointment, tension, and conflict. He was diagnosed with liver cancer while on a leave of absence from teaching painting as an associate professor of fine arts. His poor health and spirits caused him to move back to Cedar Rapids, where he died on February 12, 1942, the day before his 51st birthday.

Today Iowa City has a population of approximately 65,000. The university has an athletic rivalry with Iowa State University in Ames and distinguishes itself academically as a school with more of an emphasis on liberal arts and medical research; ISU focuses on science, agriculture, and veterinary medicine. Similar to the time of Grant Wood, Iowa City remains today a larger nexus of fine-arts training, so it is not surprising that Wood sought a teaching position at the University of Iowa above other academic institutions in the state.

Because Iowa City is near Cedar Rapids and this book hopes to suggest fuel-efficient driving routes, part 3 begins in Iowa City but then travels east to Davenport, where the Figge Art Museum houses some of Wood's paintings and those of other Midwestern Regionalist artists. It then continues south and back through time to Eldon, the site of the home from *American Gothic*,

45

Art Insight: Grant Wood's Women

Grant Wood was born to Hattie when she was 33; and he was the second child of four. His first art teacher and patron, she encouraged his drawing by supplying him with art materials and sheltering him under the kitchen table to pursue his craft when his father was skeptical of it. As an adult, Wood continued to live with his mother, who took care of his domestic needs until her heart attack and death in 1935 at the age of 77.

Wood's younger sister, Nan, born in 1899, also lived with their mother as an adult. From 1917 to 1924, she lived with them in the Cedar Rapids bungalow Wood had built for his mother. When Wood was offered the use of the carriage house loft of the Turner Mortuary in 1924, Nan and Hattie moved with him, Nan occupying the studio for 11 years until she married Edward Graham and moved to the West Coast. After Wood's death in 1942, Nan became executor of his estate and artistic legacy, and she was known in art circles for her fierce protection of his work's copyrights and her defense of his moral character to the public.

Although the Cedar Rapids press would occasionally name Wood as one of the most eligible bachelors in town, he didn't seem to make time for romance. Thus his friends were shocked when, at the age of 44, he announced his betrothal to Sara Sherman Maxon, a tall, silver-haired, flashily dressed

Hattie Weaver Wood, 1919
Image courtesy of the Figge Art Museum, Grant Wood Archive, Davenport, Iowa

woman who gave voice lessons in town. David Turner and other friends viewed the two as mismatched, but Wood appreciated how kind Sara was to his mother, who needed nursing to recuperate from a heart attack. Maxon was five years older than Wood, had a son and grandchild from a previous marriage, and had worked as an actress and opera singer. They bought the Iowa City house when they married in March 1935, and his mother lived with them briefly until her death in October of that year.

and Amana, where he painted *Young Corn* as a younger and more hopefilled man. Pausing at the Amana colonies as well as the Amish community in Kalona will provide the opportunity to see how other citizens found the freedom to envision a utopia in Iowa, and to contextualize Wood's Stone proclivities. The timing of the marriage (concurrent with his mother's inability to care for his physical needs any longer) and Wood's choice of a woman older than himself make one wonder if the marriage wasn't a practical solution (perhaps even encouraged by Wood's mother herself before she died) to ensure the artist would have his domestic needs met so his artistic work could continue. Wood and Maxon divorced in 1939 after four years of marriage, and she lived out the rest of her life on the West Coast.

Grant and Nan in the parlor of his Iowa City home. Image courtesy of the Cedar Rapids Museum of Art Archives

After his mother died, Wood had two men live with them: Park Rinard, who worked as his personal secretary and was ghostwriter of his unfinished autobiography, and Eric Knight, author of the children's classic *Lassie Come Home*. Recent academic research on Grant Wood has reported that the diary entries of his wife from their time in Iowa City were rife with her jealousy and disappointment over his attentions to male houseguests, and art historians speculate about Wood's possible homosexual

Grant Wood and his wife, Sara
Image courtesy of the Figge Art Museum

City colony in the spectrum of other historical communal experiments in the state.

While Davenport itself was not a stomping ground for Wood, and he did not live, paint, or teach in the city, it is an essential place to visit. The Figge's collection is useful in considering Wood at his most introspective, and it includes several of his most penetrating self-portraits, done later in life after he had completed his iconic masterpiece, *American Gothic*. Observing him in this timeless gallery of artists where each has expressed individual talent in the alchemy of paint, one can see these paintings as recorded moments filled with struggle, success, and failure. Wood's tragic sadness in his late self-portraits calls Rembrandt to mind; Rembrandt's loneliness is so well mirrored in Wood's own Iowan refuge.

The stop in Davenport also provides the traveler with the opportunity to become further acquainted with Iowa river cities and their picturesque assemblage of historic buildings. Davenport, along with Iowa city Bettendorf and Illinois cities Moline and Rock Island across the Mississippi, is part of what is known as the Quad Cities, with a total population of 400,000. Commerce along the Mississippi River has always fueled the economies of the region since its founding by French traders and missionaries. Today, the mighty Mississippi is still used as a major mode of transportation, but its shores are also a serene place to picnic, rest on one of the benches along the riverbank, and observe the grain barges, small motorboats, and bald eagles as they each slowly traverse the Mississippi in their own manner. Davenport also offers riverboat cruises, bike trails, casinos, John Deere attractions, and shopping in quaint villages, and its Hilltop Campus Village is an Iowa Main Street Urban Neighborhood District participating in the National Trust for Historic Preservation's downtown revitalization program.

For more information about Iowa City and Davenport, contact the Iowa City Visitor Center, Hayden Fry Way, Coralville, 800-283-6592, www.iowa citycoralville.org; or the Davenport Visitors Center, Union Station, 102 S. Harrison Street, Davenport, 563-322-3911, ext. 114, www.visitquadcities.com.

GRANT WOOD'S HOUSE
1142 E. Court St., Iowa City

This pre–Civil War house, by far the grandest home that Wood ever occupied, is not open to the public, but the exterior is in plain view from the sidewalk. It was the backdrop for several tragedies in his life, including the death of his mother, the struggles of an unsuccessful academic career, a failed marriage, and the onset of terminal cancer.

The Italianate home was built in 1858 by Nicholas Oakes, a brick manufacturer. The walls of the home range from 17 to 24 inches thick. During

1142 E. Court Street, ca. 1938
Image courtesy of the Figge Art Museum, Grant Wood Archive, Davenport, Iowa

the Depression, the Mr. Oakes's daughter converted the home into apart-ments and rented rooms. Grant Wood bought the home four years after gain-ing international acclaim with *American Gothic* and restored the estate back to its original floor plan. As he was trained in the Arts and Crafts movement during his education in Minnesota and Chicago and had experience building low-cost housing for his mother, he made many improvements to the home himself, fashioning a copper hood for the fireplace, building bookshelves, and adding wainscoting. After Wood's marriage, he and his wife entertained lavishly in the home, hosting dinners at a 20-foot dining-room table. The home was placed on the National Register of Historic Places in 1978.

PLUM GROVE HISTORIC HOME

1030 Carroll St., Iowa City
319-351-5738
www.iowahistory.org
/historic-sites/plum-
grove/index.html

Open 1–5 Wed.–Sun., Memorial
Day–Labor Day; 1–5 Sat. and Sun.
Labor Day–Oct. 31
Admission: free

While you can't go into some of the private homes that Wood lived in, there are several historic homes of similar vintage open to tourists. A short distance from the University of Iowa campus is the home of Iowa's first territorial governor, Robert Lucas, and his wife, Friendly, which is now open for tours. The seven-room Greek Revival home was finished in 1853 and sits on 4 acres with three historical gardens. It is listed on the National Register of Historic Places.

U OF I CAMPUS, ART MUSEUM, AND ART DEPARTMENT

University of Iowa Memorial Union
125 N. Madison St., Room 126,
Iowa City

319-335-0548
www.uiowa.edu

Grant Wood taught at the University of Iowa beginning in 1933, when he was awarded the title of associate professor of fine arts by the school. Due to damage sustained in the river flooding of 2008, the university's art department and museum are closed. As of this writing the university art collection is housed in the Figge Art Museum in Davenport (see "The Figge Art Museum"), and the art department studios were temporarily operating off campus in a former lumberyard. Please check the university's website to see if the art museum and art department have reopened when you plan your travels.

Iowa was the 29th state to join the union, in 1846.

In the meantime, be sure not to miss the old capitol building, the first state capital of Iowa, which is situated on the Pentacrest in the heart of Iowa City and the university's campus. The two-story capitol later served as the first university building and is now restored to reflect period legislative chambers and hosts changing exhibits. The few seats clustered around a potbellied stove in the chambers communicates how small government was for western territories. The gift shop and restored rooms are open 10–3 weekdays and 10–5 weekends; admission is free.

The state's first capitol building is now home to a museum and part of University of Iowa's campus. Iowa Tourism Office

AMERICAN *GOTHIC* HOUSE
300 *American Gothic St., Eldon*

The second most eminent white house in America is located in Eldon, Iowa, a town of 1,700 people located on IA 16, southwest of Davenport and Iowa City. While visitors tour the White House in Washington, DC, out of respect for the global power wielded there, pilgrims to the *American Gothic* home, made of wood and reclaimed church windows, come because they are intrigued by the tension and humility of the figures and setting of the painting. The artwork has become an international testament for the reverence of humanity in its workaday plodding. The iconographic painting, packed with cultural commentary, ushered in American Modernism.

The history of the painting began in 1930, when Grant Wood was invited to lead a plein air painting demonstration in Eldon at an experimental gallery, library, and art school established by Edward Rowan, a Harvard graduate who had been recruited to Iowa by the Palmer family and directed the Little Gallery in Cedar Rapids. Wood came upon the house, which had been built in 1881 by local carpenters Busey and Herald, and asked Mrs. Rowan to take photographs of it for him. He immediately began talking about the vertical lines of the home and how he would place elongated figures in front of it to

The home that inspired American Gothic Iowa Tourism Office

Nan Wood-Graham and Dr. B. H. McKeeby pose next to American Gothic, *Art Institute of Chicago, ca. 1942* Cedar Rapids Museum of Art Archives

repeat the geometry. For the figures, Wood thought to convey a sentiment of protectiveness of a farmer for his spinster daughter (though many people erroneously assume they are a married couple), and he had the ideal models in mind: his dentist for the farmer, and an actual spinster in Cedar Rapids for the daughter. He didn't feel confident asking the spinster to pose, however, out of concern for offending the woman, so instead he asked his sister, Nan. She agreed and dressed in the same sort of house clothes in which he had his mother pose for *Woman with Plants.*

Wood wrote that he made sketches and planned a composition that would purposefully elongate the human features to match the vertical stretches of the windows. Was it the architectural shorthand of the Gothic arched windows that prompted Wood to want to communicate real belief in transcendental opportunities experienced in the common person's life, or was he good-humoredly critiquing the narrowness and confines of small-town living, where parameters for life are parsed out frugally?

While the home is a private residence and not open to the public, the town has opened the **American Gothic House Center** (300 American Gothic St., Eldon; 641-652-3352; www.americangothichouse.net; 10–5 Tues.–Sat. and 1–4 Sun.–Mon., May–Sept.; 10–4 Tues.–Fri. and 1–4 Sat.–Mon., Oct.–Apr.; free admission) just steps away from the home. The center includes a parodies exhibit, a media room with educational films about Grant Wood, and a gift shop. It also rents costumes to tourists, who pose for pictures in front of the house. As Eldon has changed very little since 1930, watching the tourists photograph themselves is the principal amusement in town.

AMISH COMMUNITY IN KALONA

Located 19 miles southwest   *www.kalonaiowa.org*
of Iowa City off US 218

The **Amish and Mennonites** began settling in Iowa in the 1860s, and they've maintained their practices of piety and simplicity since then, including forsaking use of rubber tires and many machines with engines, such as automobiles and tractors. Be careful of slow moving black carriages and children on horseback as you drive around Kalona. If you explore the gravel roads around Kalona for a few miles, you will see tidy gardens, hand-painted signs for eggs and other farm products, and children modestly dressed in identical garb as their parents. Year-round you can rub elbows with the Amish as they do their shopping at one of the general stores in Kalona, and you can peruse the hundreds of handmade quilts on display, including many by local Amish and Mennonite women, at the annual **Kalona Quilt Show and Sale** (for more information call 319-656-2240).

Folk art in the form of barn hex signs is plentiful in Washington County. Reportedly, there are more per square mile than in any other county in the United States. The locals call them "barn quilts," and there is a self-guided tour and map online at www.barnquilts iowa.com. The county seat, Washington, is a vibrant slice of Americana, with a band shell, Victorian storefronts, and a Saturday morning market.

Be sure not to miss the **Kalona Historical Village** (715 D Ave., Kalona; 319-656-3232; www.kalonaiowa.org; 9:30–4 Mon.–Sat., Apr.–Oct.; 11–3 Mon.–Sat., Nov.–Mar.). The complex of restored buildings includes a Mennonite museum and archives, an Amish museum, a textile museum, two homes, a country store, and a one-room schoolhouse. The same organization offers bus tours of the countryside and shopping, which leave from 514 B

Quilts for sale in Kalona   Iowa Tourism Office

Avenue Monday through Saturday from April to October. Prices vary for the tours, as there is a choice of customized routes. Advanced reservations are necessary.

 THE AMANA COLONIES

Amana Heritage Museum,
Community Church, and
Agriculture Museum
4310 220th Trail, Amana
319-622-3567

www.amanaheritage.org
Open 10–5 Mon.–Sat. and noon–4
Sun., Apr.–Oct.; 10–5 Sat., Nov.–Mar.
Admission: $7 adults, children free
with adult admission

If you return to I-80 from Kalona and are headed west toward Des Moines or Ames, you can easily make a small detour on the exit marked for the Amanas. Just a few miles off I-80, the Amana Colonies offer a fascinating story of the German settlers who immigrated to Iowa together in 1855 and then successfully worked the land for several generations. They created an entirely self-sufficient religious utopia with seven villages that included communal dormitories and work spaces.

Grant Wood and his young apprentice Lee Allen sketched at the Amana Colonies on many occasions in the 1930s. The two met when Allen won first prize at the Iowa State Fair in 1929. Allen became an important Midwestern Regionalist in his own right, and his work is in the collections of the University of Iowa Museum and the Figge Art Museum. You will recognize the rolling hills and verdant green of the countryside of their paintings as you tour this cluster of villages.

Today the villages have been collectively designated a National Historic Landmark. Many descendants of the settlers still live and farm in the Amanas, but the communal buildings are no longer used for church families and instead are restored as museums, shops, and restaurants. The Heritage Museum occupies three of the colony's buildings and presents exhibits on the settlers' daily life and religious practices, including a well-made film. Also in the vicinity and open to tour are agricultural buildings and a church. The **Amana Community Church Museum** (4210 V St., Homestead) has hosts who explain the religious beliefs of the founders, and the **Communal Agriculture Museum** (505 P St., South Amana) is housed in an 1860 barn. The architecture and agricultural practices and equipment showcased in the museum resemble the type of agrarian childhood memories that Wood painted.

THE FIGGE ART MUSEUM

1737 W. 12th St., Davenport
563-326-7804
www.figgeartmuseum.org
Open 10–5 Tues.–Sat. (until 9 on Thurs.), noon–5 Sun.

Admission: $7 adults, $6 seniors and students with ID, $4 children under 12; free admission for seniors first Thurs. of the month

East of Iowa city, Davenport is the home of the Figge Art Museum, a substantial and impressive building of more than 100,000 square feet that sits a virtual stone's throw from the Mississippi River. It is worth a visit just to see the museum building, which is the work of an important and up-and-coming British architect, David Chipperfield. Vast and well laid out, it is

The Figge Art Museum resembles a
modern-day crystal palace.
Image courtesy of the Figge Art Museum,
Grant Wood Archive, Davenport, Iowa

The Regionalist gallery installation at
the Figge   Image courtesy of the Figge Art
Museum, Grant Wood Archive, Davenport, Iowa

mostly made of glass and is typically English in its understated subtlety. It is quite extraordinary to have such a museum in a rather small Midwestern town, instead being something one would expect to see in San Francisco, Atlanta, or some other culturally progressive city. It suggests that Iowans take culture seriously, invest in it, and take the time to research the very best of the new.

There are more than 3,500 works of art in the museum's permanent collection and multiple temporary gallery exhibitions. The permanent collection features Thomas Hart Benton and other Midwestern Regionalist school of painters, as well as Iowan artists such as Harold Bloom, John Steuart Curry, and Grant Wood. Temporary exhibitions have included the John Deere Art Collection, a superb exhibition entitled "Dancing Towards Death: The Richard Harris Collection," and "A Legacy for Iowa: Pollack's Mural and Masterworks from the UIMA." The latter, from the University of Iowa, was on temporary display due to the devastating 2008 flood in Iowa City that destroyed the university art museum. Controversy has ensued because the university considered selling the Pollack mural—one of the most valuable works in the world—in order to finance a new museum.

The two Wood self-portraits in the collection offer the opportunity to view him in a particularly personal light. If visiting Cedar Rapids, the place that celebrated him and welcomed him home, is a way to understand his life and values, then this trip to Davenport and the Figge Art Museum offers a different view, a glimpse of Wood's more private feelings about himself and his fellow Iowans in psychological self-portraits that could be seen as confessionals or cultural critiques. The two self-portraits are a must-see, and descriptions follow.

Return from Bohemia (1935), Grant Wood

This elaborately painted work was intended by Wood to act as the cover for a planned book, a memoir he had been writing with the assistance of his friend Park Rinard. The book title was to have been Return from Bohemia, and the illustrated scene reflects the title. It shows Wood in front of his Iowa brethren, having forsaken his bohemian aspirations in Paris. He sets himself in a completely Midwestern scene, in front of a red barn and with a group of rather typical farmers and plain-suited folk. These figures do not look out at the viewer, or apparently at the painting on Wood's canvas; rather they appear to have their eyes closed, almost as if they are in some kind of trance. Their downward-looking posture and their closed eyes recall the sculptures of Christian Petersen in Ames (see part 4). One can only begin to speculate as to the reasons why. Is it the sadness of their lives that makes them so unable to look up, or is there some secret that we know nothing about, some impenetrable and ghastly event that has forced this group to look so downcast? Could the image be reminiscent of Goya's *The Sleep of Reason,* in which there exists a menacing conflict between the human and the degradation of consciousness, or are these figures merely looking downward because of their humility?

In contrast, Wood seems to reveal himself; he looks directly at the viewer, his eyes serious and focused, looking determined and even ambitious. The figures behind him are collaged and don't seem to actually occupy the same space, though they are painted as he is (with almost photographic realism), and yet the spatial logic of the scene is inconsistent and does not add up. Here Wood is seen as the protagonist of a downtrodden and psychologically haunted populace. Only Wood looks up to face reality heroically and redeem a disenfranchised society—the artist as savior, or as Grant's contemporary Cecil Collins contended, "artist as priest hierophant."

Self-Portrait (1932–1941), Grant Wood

The reflection upon the self is perhaps the most psychologically challenging task a painter can undertake, and this small painting shows Wood at his most sincere and intimate. It is rendered in an extremely meticulous way and reveals him in an isolated world with only fields and a lone windmill behind him. The painting suggests none of the defiance and ambition of *Return from Bohemia;* rather, his eyes are slightly bloodshot, and his expression seems almost tired. The painting is a testament to the great Flemish painters of the medieval age who could paint every hair on a man's head, and whom Wood greatly admired. It reveals in a certain sense the face of a warrior, a person determined to overcome obstacles and to be able to see life and his own physical form objectively—that is, to see the concrete shapes and colors of a physiognomy as it exists in all its detail.

The solitude of the fields seem symbolic of Wood's growing isolation as his type of regional art was increasingly seen as outmoded. At the time he created this painting, his personal ambitions to operate on a larger sphere as an artist by living in Europe were thoroughly finished, and he painted his own visage in a matter-of-fact, straightforward fashion. It is a painting that attempts to enter the history of painting, with Wood's face staring out from the mysterious eternity of the painter's world. It has all the depth of feeling and content of a Rembrandt or a Van Gogh self-portrait.

TODAY'S LANDSCAPE
Ancillary Art and Ecoattractions

Iowa City Farmer's Market
Downtown Iowa City
319-356-5210
www.icgov.org/farmersmarket
Open 5:30–7:30 PM Wed. and 7:30–noon Sat., May–Oct.

A wonderful cornucopia of products are on offer, including bread, meats, and organic produce grown by local farmers, and there are educational forums on the benefit of locally grown products and how they can enhance quality of life. You can park at Chauncey Swan Parking Ramp across from City Hall on East Washington Street.

Iowa Arts Festival
Iowa City
www.summerofthearts.org

Since 1987, Iowa City has hosted a summer arts festival that spans seven blocks and includes more than 120 artists and live performers. The dates for

the festival vary each year, so check
online.

Riverside Theatre
213 N. Gilbert St., Iowa City
319-338-7672
www.riversidetheatre.org

From September through April,
this professional community theater
presents classics, musicals, and new
plays. Outside summer season performances are held in Lower City
Park. Schedules are available on
their website.

Hancher Auditorium
W317 Seashore Hall, University
of Iowa, Iowa City
319-335-1160
www.hancher.uiowa.edu

*Downtown Iowa City hosts street festivals and
farmers markets. The annual Jazz Festival hosts
jazz from around the world.*   Iowa Tourism Office

University-organized events are held here, including touring Broadway
shows, ballet, opera, symphony, and pop concerts.

Riverboat Ride on the *Celebration Belle*
2501 River Dr., Moline, Illinois
309-764-1952 or 800-297-0034
www.celebrationbelle.com

A Mississippi River paddleboat cruise is an excellent way to enter into the
Iowan landscape at its eastern border with Illinois. The landscape and architectural views today are largely the same as those that Grant Wood and his
parents would have witnessed a hundred years ago. Various companies operate
cruises on the Mississippi, but the *Celebration Belle* has several cruise options
and is the largest noncasino excursion vessel on the Mississippi. The company
offers a full-day cruise with three meals and live performances, or shorter nar-
rated and themed cruises including fall foliage tours, Oktoberfest, and big
band dinner dances. They also have a two-day / overnight package.

Grant Wood Scenic Byway
http://iowadot.gov/iowasbyways
This rural drive starts along the Mississippi in Bellevue and has signs posted
to lead motorists through the small towns of Springbrook, Andrew,
Maquoketa, Baldwin, Monmouth, and Wyoming to end up at Grant Wood's
birthplace, Anamosa, and then on to Stone City. If you want to start your

Grant Wood tour in Davenport, at the eastern end of the state, consider taking this route to reach Anamosa.

Davenport Farmer's Market
Historic Freight House
421 W. River Dr., Davenport
Open 3–6 Tues. and 8–1 Sat., year-round

The farmer's market operates indoors and outdoors, weather permitting. The Victorian building is an interesting setting for the candy, wine, salsa, dog treats, and even massage services that are on offer.

River Music Experience Museum
131 W. Second St., Davenport
877-326-1333
www.rivermusicexperience.org
Open 7–7 Mon., 7 AM–9 PM Tues. and Thurs.–Fri.,
7 AM–10 PM Wed., 10–9 Sat., and 10–5 Sun.
Admission: free

Weather permitting, the River Music Experience Museum hosts free concerts on the plaza adjacent to the museum's main entrance and presents all the varieties of music that evolved and flourished along the Mississippi. Please visit the museum's website to see the concert schedule and information about special exhibitions.

Bix Beiderbecke Jazz Festival
Various venues in downtown Davenport
888-249-5487
www.bixsociety.org

This annual summertime festival is staged in honor of Davenport's legendary hometown musician, Bix Beiderbecke, who was born in Davenport in the 1890s. Held since the 1970s, the festival's free concerts feature visiting traditional jazz bands from around the country at four venues, including LeClaire Park on the Mississippi riverfront. The schedule for the current year is on the festival website.

Vander Veer Botanical Park and Conservatory
215 W. Central Park Ave., Davenport
563-326-7818
www.cityofdavenportiowa.com
vvbp-education@mchsi.com
Open 10–4 Tues.–Sun., year-round
Admission: $1 adults, free for children under 16 for the
conservatory only; free for all for the botanical park

River boat cruises are the quintessential way to experience the redolent grandeur of the Mississippi   Iowa Tourism Office

This historic botanical park has a conservatory and growing house, outdoor gardens, fountains, and sculptures. Don't miss the nationally recognized rose garden and hosta glade.

Mississippi River Visitor Center on Arsenal Island
Take Government Bridge from Davenport
across the river to Rock Island Arsenal
309-794-5338
www.missriver.org
Open 9–5 daily
Admission: free

Arsenal Island features a Confederate cemetery, the Arsenal Museum, and Colonel Davenport's home, and there is a free tour of the lock and dam system offered on summer weekends at 11 and 2. Advance reservations must be made for the tour, and the army requires you to display identification when you enter the premises.

Fairfield First Fridays Art Walk
641-233-8883
www.fairfieldartwalk.org

The first Friday of the month, a sponsored open house is held at every gallery and art venue in Fairfield, with each month featuring a different theme. Fairfield counts more than 200 visual and performing artists as residents.

Wineries

There are a couple of wineries in the area:

Cedar Valley Winery (Dewberry Ave., Battavia; 641-662-2860; www.cedarvalleywine.com). Quality hybrid French and American wines produced on a 6-acre vineyard.

Crane Winery (11420 Main St., Selma; 641-936-4355; www.crane winery.com). The sweetest little winery of southwest Iowa has a tasting room in their Van Buren County haven.

FARTHER AFIELD

Tipton Carnegie Public Library
206 Cedar St., Tipton
563-886-6266
www.tipton.lib.ia.us
Open 10–8 Mon.–Thurs.,
10–5 Fri., and 10–1 Sat.
Admission: free

The Tipton Carnegie Public Library dates from 1903 and proudly exhibits 21 of Grant Wood's lithographs, as well as works by his colleague and friend Marvin Cone.

Iowa still sports hundreds of century old wooden barns like the ones in Regionalist paintings Iowa Tourism Office

There is also a Soldiers Monument on the front lawn, which commemorates Cedar County residents who have lost their lives in service to their country.

Dubuque Museum of Art
701 Locust St., Dubuque
563-557-1851
www.dbqart.com
Open 10–5 Tues.–Fri., 1–4 Sat.–Sun.; closed Thanksgiving,
Christmas, and New Year's Day
Admission: free

North of Davenport on the Mississippi River, Dubuque is a charming river town frozen in time. The Dubuque art museum has more than 2,100 works in its permanent collection, including those by John Steuart Curry and Grant Wood. On long-term loan is Wood's *Appraisal* (1931). This is a piece not to be missed, as well as *Iowa Autumn, Indian Creek* (1924–1926), a most delightful landscape. There are visiting exhibitions and works by local artists as well.

National Mississippi River Museum and Aquarium
350 E. Third St., Dubuque
800-226-3369
www.mississippirivermuseum.com
Open 9–6 daily, Memorial Day weekend–Labor Day;
9–5 daily, Labor Day–October 31; 10–5 daily,
November–Memorial Day weekend
Admission: $15 adults, $12 seniors, and $10 youth,
with discounts offered online

A worthwhile attraction, the National Mississippi River Museum and Aquarium, in association with the Smithsonian Institution, displays 10 large aquariums, historic riverboats that can be boarded, the National River Hall of Fame, and a 3-D movie theater.

Mark Twain Boyhood Home and Museum
120 N. Main St., Hannibal, Missouri
573-221-9010
www.marktwainmuseum.org
Open 9–5 daily
Admission: $10 adults, $8.50 seniors, $6 children six
and older, free for children under six

At the Mark Twain Boyhood Home and Museum, located 110 miles south of Davenport, you can tour historic buildings, see temporary traveling exhibitions, and view film screenings of adaptations of his writing.

Art Institute of Chicago
111 S. Michigan Ave., Chicago, Illinois
312-443-3600 or 877-307-4242
www.artinstituteofchicago.org
Open 10:30–5 Sun.–Wed. and Fri.–Sat., 10:30–8 Thurs.
Admission: $18 adults; $12 students, youth, and seniors

If your voyage can start farther east or you have additional time, *American Gothic* is on display at this fabulous treasure trove of art, which is located two hours east of the Mississippi River in Illinois on the shores of Lake Michigan.

Grant Wood's Midsummer *(1929) depicts an Iowa landscape that has not changed much over time.* Oil on canvas, 28¼ x 36¾ in., Museum purchase, Save-the-art fund. 2007.040b. Cedar Rapids Museum of Art

4 AMES
Leadership in Public Art

Mural Painting is obviously well adapted to Government projects, and it is also highly suitable for regional expression. It enables students to work in groups, to develop original ideas under proper guidance, and to work with a definite purpose. . . . There is sure to be a wonderful development in mural painting within the next few years.

—GRANT WOOD,
REVOLT AGAINST THE CITY

This section focuses on the role Grant Wood played in the creation of public art (rather than easel painting). It explores his contributions to this field through his role as the Iowa director of the Public Works of Art Project (PWAP) in the 1930s and the murals he designed for Parks Library at Iowa State University, and it further explores other artists who worked alongside him on these public art projects and the status of public art and university sponsorship as it has evolved in Iowa since Wood's time. This is a great opportunity to view the legacy of Wood and his generation at the university level in the state of Iowa. With the exception of the last two, all of the attractions in this section are focused on Iowa State University.

After Wood became nationally established with *American Gothic,* he was considered a major mover and shaker in the art world, and his evolving theories concerning Regionalism were considered more seriously. His success also led to his leadership in the community. Iowa State University (ISU), together with the Roosevelt

Main Street, Ames, 1913 Courtesy of Ames Chamber of Commerce

administration, decided to put the recently successful and famous Wood to the test with a series of projects, which included the directorship of the PWAP in Iowa and a series of murals to be painted for the library on the ISU Ames campus. Part of his duties was to supervise other artists in a bold new creative regime, and the role he adopted would reinforce his theories concerning Regionalism, agriculture, and the role of art in the community. His close friend Edward Rowan from Cedar Rapids had been made assistant director of the PWAP at the national level in Washington, DC, so Wood now had the chance to work with public backing and funding, and to organize a small army of artists in America, rather than in Europe. Wood had been criticized for having used German artists for the fabrication of the Veterans Memorial window in Cedar Rapids (see the "Veterans Memorial Building Stained-Glass Window" in chapter 2), and he selected an all American crew for the work he was commissioned to do in Ames.

Ames has the second-highest number of PhDs per capita in the country. Famous as a picturesque, self-contained land grant college, ISU's contemporary vision for itself vacillates between the charm of a nurturing 19th-century university campus laid out according to Beaux-Arts planning strategies (which recall many other U.S. campuses, including Michigan State University and Berkeley in California) versus that of a thoroughly modern research complex where private chemical and seed companies underwrite salaries and grants. Ames contends that the university and nearby research park generate the second-highest number of patents nationally, lagging only behind MIT. The university is committed to the fields of agronomy, horticulture, and genetic engineering, and was the scene of a lesser-publicized role during World War

II in which labs in Ames and Los Alamos, California, conducted nuclear weapons research. It's the perfect place to confront the spectacle of transformation in American society: from the world of provincial farmers and pioneers to the society of world rulers, the inner collapse of empire, and the collaboration of science, big business, and government. It is also a place where one can see contemporary artists respond to contemporary issues in expressive, independent, and politically courageous ways.

The university hosts an impressive collection of art created for the public, including several murals painted by Wood and commissioned by the university as part of the PWAP, as well as a large quantity of sculptures created by Wood's contemporary Christian Petersen. Additionally, there are numerous other works of public art on the campus, including the campus "art walk," which is an indirect result of the legacy of the PWAP. A thriving contemporary art sponsorship still exists, and it is possible to view new and emerging artists, the Grant Woods of our time. The university's Brunnier Art Museum, housed in a vast 1960s concrete building, has a good collection of Iowa art, including several of Wood's contemporaries.

Farmers sell fresh-picked goodies at one of Ames's outdoor farmer's markets
Ames Chamber of Commerce

Outside of the university, in the city of Ames there are also examples of public art projects, including the post office mural paintings of the 1930s executed by Lowell Houser, who worked under the PWAP directorship of Grant Wood. The state of Iowa has more than 40 post office murals and paintings, most of them commissioned by the state-funded programs of the Great Depression. This powerful example of Depression-era murals, along with the architecture of the post office that houses them, is particularly impressive.

Aside from the artwork, downtown Ames is full of character and exudes a grounded atmosphere of times gone by. There are several interesting churches in the vicinity and a stereotypically wide western-U.S. main street, spacious enough for a team of horses to turn a wagon in front of the redbrick-facade stores. The whole town rattles and shakes

Festival, downtown Ames
Ames Chamber of Commerce

when the immensely long Union and Pacific trains pass a block away from Main Street on the most active rail line in the country. On a visit to Ames one can enjoy first-class entertainment and recreation all year long, including enjoying one of its festivals or farmer's markets, visiting the award-winning Reiman Botanical Gardens, taking in touring Broadway musicals, seeing popular concerts, and going to ISU Cyclone games. Ames is a "Main Street Iowa" community participating in the National Trust for Historic Preservation's downtown revitalization program.

For more information about Ames, contact the Ames Convention and Visitors Bureau, 1601 Golden Aspen Drive, Suite 110, Ames; 515-232-4032800-288-7470; www.visitames.com.

PARKS LIBRARY: *Grant Wood Murals and Christian Petersen Sculpture*

Parks Library, Iowa State   515-294-3642
University   www.lib.iastate.edu
Corner of Osborn Dr. and
Morrill Rd., Ames

When Tillage Begins, Other Arts Follow (1933–1934) and *Breaking the Prairie Sod* (1935–1937), Grant Wood

Located in the Parks Library, this impressive group of murals were designed by Wood and then executed with the assistance of a team of painters provided for him through the PWAP. They are an iconic expression of a time that is becoming ever more remote and provide a glimpse of Wood's artistic temperament.

The more ambitious work, *When Tillage Begins, Other Arts Follow* is located on the walls of an impressive stair that links the ground floor of the library to the first floor. The murals are also accessible through the modern wing of the library, but the original sequence will be disrupted, so it is better to visit the paintings by first seeing the lower level. The current arrangement of the library doesn't facilitate the scheme of the mural cycle (as mural projects are often called), as Wood organized the murals much like a European artist of the 15th century would have; that is, he intended to tell a story. There is a narrative structure, and its depth is complex. The mural occupies three walls and integrates delightfully with the classical architecture of the stairwell.

The theme of the work and its title come from Daniel Webster's notion, fully quoted, "When tillage begins, other arts follow. The farmers, therefore, are the founder of human civilization"—a theme quite appropriate to an agricultural-, science-, and technology-focused university, and a theme important to the formation of a new society searching for the basis upon which to construct itself. As a monumental representation it can be seen as the collective expression of a new country defining itself and the roles of its members. The project is an attempt to organize society and to teach a moral code through the dutiful appreciation of daily habits and gender-specific roles. It visually demonstrates the roles of man, nature, and machine, and can be seen as prophetic in content.

In *Breaking the Prairie Sod,* the first image of the group, a man looking much like Abraham Lincoln stops plowing to drink while other men chop trees on the two side panels. Students of Wood's executed the mural, and it was created after the paintings on the upper level. The iconography of the work seems simple enough and responds to the notion of the farmer and pioneer carving out the way for civilization to follow. There are quite profound interpretations of the work depending how far one is willing to delve into the psychology and symbolism of the painting. The trees in the side panels do not seem part of an enormous forest, but rather are lonely; they could in fact be representational of the tree of life, and their placement in the corners of the space suggest their necessity as columns in the architectural sequence. They are, however, being cut down, making way for a dominant horizontality in which all architectural reference is forgotten and the two central figures of man and woman echo Adam and Eve. The intense tension of the work thus suggests all kinds of undercurrents reiterated by the lack of natural light in the space and the almost hyper-precise painting style.

On the upper level of the stair are three schemes: *Agriculture, Home Economics,* and *Engineering.* These are organized in a gender-specific way, with the roles of both sexes being defined (women work in the home / men go outside to farm, to put it crassly).

The figures are about life-size, and the murals themselves are painted on canvas and mounted with glue onto the wall, rather than being directly painted on its surface. The effect is somewhere between that of a high school art project and a quattrocento Italian fresco for a medieval church. Wood laid out the scheme for each mural in small scale, and the oil sketch he made for the triptych of panels entitled *Agriculture,* which includes the themes of veterinary medicine, farm crops, and husbandry, is on display at the Cedar Rapids Museum of Art (see part 2).

Wood and his large team of assistants worked out everything in detail using this small oil sketch as a basis. He used models to create full-scale drawings on brown paper (a practice he had become accustomed to during the creation of the Veterans Memorial stained-glass window—see part 2), and these drawings were worked out in full detail. The assistants Wood selected were expected to execute the designs exactly the way in which he had made them, and the process was systematic and precise. Wood organized the team much like a bottega of the Italian Renaissance, with each assistant responsible for a given task. For instance, his friend Arnold Pyle mixed paint and was expected to make precise color alignments.

Library Girl and Boy (1944), Christian Petersen

Christian Petersen became campus sculptor at roughly the same time Wood began the library murals. Petersen has work dotted about the campus in a similar way to which the work of Michelangelo is dotted about Florence. The two pieces here, also located in the library, are approximately life-size and weave into the architectural setting of the stair, hall, and murals in a powerful and rhetorical fashion. There is a strange downcast posture to both figures, which the student body says is due to tentative flirtation. This downward and rather introspective quality is an emblematic characteristic of Petersen's work. The two figures have a surreal quality and seem almost alive, trapped in a state of preoccupied and studious agony that is further heightened by the strong academic delineation of the sculptor's technique.

MORRILL HALL AND THE CHRISTIAN PETERSEN ART MUSEUM

Morrill Hall, Iowa State University
Morrill Rd., Ames

515-294-3342
www.museums.iastate.edu /CPAM.html

Entrance to Morrill Hall
William Balthazar Rose

Morrill Hall dates from the 19th century and houses a temporary exhibition space, lecture halls, and the Christian Petersen Art Museum. The redbrick building is vaguely Romanesque Revival in character. The Petersen museum is in the basement and alternates exhibitions of Petersen's works with temporary shows of other artists.

The museum can be approached by climbing massive stairs to its front or by accessing the much more alluring side entry behind the student café. If you choose the latter, several Petersen sculptures are immediately visible. All created on a small scale, these bronze pieces are arranged on standing plinths that march alongside the entry path to the museum.

The figures exhibit the typical thorough academic skill of Petersen, and they are delightful to see, as they are both intimate in scale and unexpected. One is immediately reminded of just how much more pleasant life is when a little art is included! Inside the building, several more works by Petersen dot the halls. Changing exhibitions are on the second floor.

Art Insight: Great Inspiration in the Great Depression
The Public Works of Art Project (PWAP)

The PWAP was one of several public art projects sponsored by the government during the presidency of Franklin Roosevelt. It was highly successful and called on local artists to lend their talents to public work, specifically to provide the embellishment of public buildings. Other such projects included the Federal Art Project (FAP) arranged by the Works Progress Administration (WPA), and the Section of Painting and Sculpture. Each had been organized as an attempt to give artists employment and were part of a larger effort to revitalize the economy after the Great Depression as part of the New Deal. Under the PWAP, for the first time artists were employed on a grand scale and treated like workmen, being paid a salary and working on projects alongside tradesmen such as plumbers and electricians. The program was a virtual renaissance for the artist, uniting him with other artists and providing all with sponsorship at a mass level. Never before and never since have artists in the United States received so much support collectively.

Grant Wood was made director of the PWAP in the state of Iowa by the overall national director, Edward Bruce, in 1933, a year before he was employed by the University of Iowa. Wood was in charge of the orchestration of the program and hiring all of the artists for it, and he established one of the most ambitious mural schemes of the project, the Parks Library Murals at Iowa State University, Ames. Wood hired local artists to work with him, including Christian Petersen (who created his own sculptural scheme), John Bloom, Arnold Pyle, Lee Allen, and Lowell Houser. The team established themselves in an unused gymnasium swimming pool on the Iowa City campus and worked on a number of projects here, including murals for the Des Moines Library (which were never completed).

Despite its success, the PAWP was short-lived, running from December 1933 to June 1934. The legacy it left was enormous, however; it employed more than 3,700 artists who created more than 15,000 works of art. Grant Wood's contribution as director for the state of Iowa resulted in murals that were rivaled only by those executed in San Francisco at Coit Tower, though his are not well-known outside of Iowa. The effects of the program are still seen today and demonstrate the power and pleasure the arts can give when properly supported at a public level. During today's age of franchises and mass-manufactured goods and homes, the hand-fashioned legacy of the PWAP is a testament to how a small investment could yield huge cultural gains.

Art Insight: Christian Petersen, the Gentle Sculptor

Christian Petersen (1885–1961) is an artist of place: He was the campus sculptor for Iowa State University, where he created, lived, and taught for almost 30 years. His work on the Ames campus has become a testament to local genius in the same way, albeit on a more minor level, as that of the sculptor Donatello, who left his mark on Renaissance Florence. Petersen's numerous sculptures on campus exhibit a wide range of capacities and interests, with themes varying from agriculture to Indian folklore to war, and techniques from terra-cotta and relief murals to stone and bronze figures modeled in the round. His vision is gentle and academic, consummate in skill, and with strong classical overtones that recall works of the ancient Greeks. Of particular note is the strange downcast posture of some of his figures, figures that seem to look inward and hold some unknowable mystery that they cannot release. They are in a pose reminiscent of the figures surrounding Grant Wood in his famous self-portrait *Return from Bohemia* at the Figge Art Museum in Davenport. In fact, Petersen's associa-

tion with Grant Wood led to his installment at Ames; he was hired by Wood to assist on a variety of projects associated with the Public Works of Art Project (PWAP), and this work attracted the notice of the university.

At the time Wood hired Petersen to join the PWAP, Petersen was facing abject poverty and did not have enough money to travel from Des Moines to participate in the program (indeed, he had to borrow it). Despite this, while Petersen did have elements of tragedy to his life, his life seems to have had less desperation and suffering than Grant Wood's. Unlike Wood, Petersen was not from Iowa, but rather an immigrant from the town of Dybbol in Denmark, where he was born in 1885.

After immigrating to the United States with his parents as a child, Petersen worked as a sculptor and in die cutting, sculpting small-scale figures and jewelry. He lived and worked in a number of states and was employed in numerous sculpture commissions. He had a good though rather academic education in the arts, studying at the Art League in New York and also the

CAMPUS ART WALK

Iowa State University
515-294-3342

www.museums.iastate.edu/
AOC.html

Iowa State University's amazing and free art walk provides the opportunity to traverse the campus and view a variety of historical and contemporary works of art, including pieces by Midwestern as well as national artists. The art walk demonstrates the university's willingness to help sponsor public art pieces, and it is a perfect venue for public sculpture. There are more than 2,000 pieces of public art on display on the campus; a self-guided virtual tour

Rhode Island School of Design. While his European background contrasts largely with Wood's Iowa roots, the two had much in common artistically, and Petersen showed little interest in returning to Europe to further his career.

His early career as a professional sculptor was quite successful, and he won the commissions for the Spanish-American War Memorial for Equity Park in Newport, Rhode Island, and numerous busts of governors and ex-governors in various eastern and Midwestern states. In contrast to his early poverty, he eventually became financially comfortable and prosperous at times after completing numerous projects, one of those rare artists who actually earn a living from their work and treat it as a job. He had everything going well for him till he divorced at the age of 43, his wife, Emma L. Hoenicke, and their three children being awarded the majority of the family assets, which left Petersen destitute.

After the divorce, he moved to Chicago, where he stayed at the YMCA and resumed work as a die caster, for the firm of Dodge and Ascher. Soon afterward he moved to Belvedere, Illinois, and established a sculpture studio, and

he remarried; however, he was continuously without money and was hospitalized for malnutrition. Things started to look up for Petersen when, through the assistance of Edgar Harlan, the curator of the State Historical Museum in Iowa, he began a series of commissions for Iowa State. The work he did for Wood and the PWAP helped to consolidate his position, and eventually he became sculptor in residence at Iowa State. Among the several important works he created for the Ames campus are the *History of Dairying* mural and the *Veterinary Medicine* mural. His luck and finances improved, Petersen became assistant professor in 1937, and his association with the college lasted until he retired at the age of 70.

What Petersen offered the Ames campus is a true eulogy, a dedication to place and to art. It represents an aspect of Regionalism in its most positive vision and confirms why regional art is important, suggesting just how close a creative being can come to arriving at profound genius. The distance from places of fame is unimportant; what is, is the dedication to art and to community, which was fostered both by Christian Petersen and his patrons.

with 40 of the artworks on an interactive map and online fact sheets is available at www.museums.iastate.edu/AOCfactsheets.html.

Grant Wood's *Breaking the Prairie Sod* and *When Tillage Begins, Other Arts Follow* are on the art walk, as well as Christian Petersen's *Library Girl and Boy* (see "Parks Library"). There are numerous additional Petersen sculptures on the art walk, including *4H Calf, Conversations, Fountain of the Four Seasons* (see "Memorial Union: Fountain and Veterans Memorial"), *Gentle Doctor, Marriage Ring, Joy, Madonna of the Prairie, Three Athletes, History of Dairying,* and *George Washington Carver.*

Other art walk sculptures by contemporary American artists that are particularly moving include the following:

Border Crossing (1989), Luis Jimenez

This particularly strong political sculpture is glazed in bright colors. The piece stands out like a shocking totem pole on a flat campus lawn not far from the library. A relentlessly vertical piece, it is a dramatic eulogy to the intrepid illegal immigrants who have searched for entry to the United States. The emotional depiction of the three figures is a memorial to the artist's grandparents, who risked everything to traverse the U.S. border, and it is dedicated to his grandfather. It is a work of hope and attempts to redress great sadness. Despite Iowa's northern location far from the Mexican border, it is home to many Latin American immigrants, and immigration is a politically charged local issue. It is encouraging to see that the university is willing to house works of art that may be in direct opposition to national policy in order to stimulate dialogue.

Left-Sided Angel (1986), Stephen De Staebler

Located to the side of the main entry to Parks Library, this sculpture offers a chance to become acquainted with the work of a most notable West Coast artist. Like the work of his contemporary Jack Zajac, De Staebler's piece has a decidedly Italian influence, resulting from a mutual interest in the preserved remains of Pompeian figures. The piece is highly dramatic, revealing a lively and dynamic approach to the process of sculpture making.

The sculpture begs the question: Is an angel with one wing capable of flight?

Jack Trice (1988), Christopher Bennett

Outside the northeast entrance of the football stadium, this sculpture pays homage to Jack Trice, ISU's first African American athlete. Determined to make a good impression, he died in 1923 from untreated injuries sustained at his first football game.

The Moth (2006), Mac Adams

This sculpture adorns the exterior of Coover Hall, the computer science building. It is a reference to the term *computer bug*, based on a researcher's discovery of a moth in a malfunctioning computer. Iowa State University claims to have invented the personal computer.

Veterinary Medicine Mural and The Gentle Doctor (1935–1938), Christian Petersen

One of the most spectacular bits of public sculpture on the campus, *The Gentle Doctor* is made of terra-cotta and is currently on display at the Veterinary Medicine Building. The mural behind it exhibits a clear homage to Greek sculpture, in particular the Elgin Marbles. The sculpture is over 7 feet tall and expresses the close bond between animals and men. It is recognized throughout the veterinary world as a symbol of the profession.

MEMORIAL UNION
Fountain and Veterans Memorial

Memorial Union, Iowa
State University
2229 Lincoln Way, Ames

515-296-6848 or 515-294-3342
www.mu.iastate.edu

If the voyager has by this point developed an interest in Wood's contemporaries, the Memorial Union student union building on the ISU campus will offer a further delight, as there are several Christian Petersen sculptures there. The Memorial Union is a large and somewhat labyrinthine affair housing all sorts of student convenience shops, meeting rooms, and lounges perfumed by the distinct smell of student cafeteria food. There are also charming vintage hotel accommodations in the building.

Fountain of the Four Seasons
(1941), Christian Petersen

Made of Bedford limestone, the fountain is part of the university's art walk (see the "Campus Art Walk" section). Located in front of the top entrance to the Union, the circular pool features four female Native Americans of the Osage tribe. Facing north, south, east, and west, they represent a chant of thanksgiving that goes somewhat like this: "Lo, I come to the tender planting. Lo, a tender shoot breaks forth." The figures

The entrance foyer to the Veterans Room in Memorial Union William Balthazar Rose

serenely squat round the pool, nurturing life through four seasons. The solemn shamanistic aura of his sculptural work stands out in contrast to the everyday student joviality milling around it.

Price of Victory (Fallen Soldier) (1944), Christian Petersen

A sanctuary inside the Union is the Veterans Room, dedicated to the valiant members of the armed forces. The quiet lounge is filled with flags and other paraphernalia, and at its center are Petersen's remarkable two GIs, cast in bronze.

POST OFFICE MURALS
525 Kellogg Ave., Ames   *515-232-1113*

Iowa State University (ISU) isn't the only place in Ames with artwork on display. The Ames post office, just off Main Street in the center of downtown, provides a most exciting and pleasant side trip. The building has a fine Doric pediment carved in gray stone and a grand entry stair that is elegant yet not overwhelming; the small-town feel of the building is reminiscent of the 1930s. Inside, the main hall boasts two large figure murals on the north wall,

The charming entrance portico of the Ames Post Office   William Balthazar Rose

which are almost identical in composition though they have been inverted. Their effect is powerful and adds to the general architectural interest of the space. The staff is friendly and courteous, even rather chatty. They seem proud of the murals and will offer a photocopied description. The lobby is open for P.O. box access after regular business hours, so you can still see the murals if you come in the evening.

The two murals were painted in 1936 by Lowell Houser (1902–1971), who worked for a period under the supervision of Wood in the Public Works of Art Project (PWAP). Wood highly respected Houser and was keen to have him on his team to create the murals designed for the Parks Library at ISU. Houser was an Ames local even though he was born in Chicago and spent his later years in California, he graduated from high school in Ames and taught at ISU.

The post office murals represent Houser at his most incisive and philosophical. The composition contrasts an Indian in front of a pyramid temple with a contemporary (1930s) Iowa farmer in front of an assem-

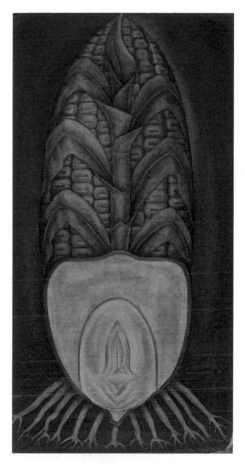

Detail of corn in the post office mural
Ames Chamber of Commerce

blage of modern building components. The narrative contrast of the two paintings is extremely strong, providing an almost dialectical structure in which philosophical and historical suggestions run rampant. The pyramid recalls the temples of the Mayans, and the Indian's pose is exactly that of the farmer opposite. The strict symmetry seems almost oppressive. The two scenes, entitled *The Evolution of Corn,* trace the historic evolution of the grain's production. The visual juxtaposition is so powerful that it rhetorically asks the viewer to delve into the monumental historical cycles of the Americas and to confront notions of civilization in a broad and penetrating manner. Further, the paintings have spiritual ramifications in their direct oppositional contrast that suggest a palimpsest of values for the contemporary art appreciator.

Houser is known to have traveled to Chichén Itzá in the Yucatán and to have made studies of pre-Columbian art. He also built a boat and traveled to Haiti. The post office murals suggest the influence of Diego Rivera, whose work he studied, and also the influence of Paul Gauguin in its overt interest in tribal and indigenous culture.

TODAY'S LANDSCAPE
Ancillary Art and Ecoattractions

Octagon Center for the Arts
427 Douglas Ave., Ames
515-232-5331
www.octagonarts.org
Exhibits open 11–3 Tues.–Fri., 1–6 Sat.
Admission: free

Named after its original location in an octagonal Victorian home, the community art center has studio spaces, galleries, and shops selling local art. The organization hosts the annual Octagon Art Festival in the summer, which is staged outside on Main Street. (Dates vary each year, so check the website.) If you're walking to the Octagon Center from the post office, take note of the lovely bronze fountain of Icarus at the intersection of Kellogg and Fifth streets.

The busy Octagon Art Festival in downtown Ames   Ames Chamber of Commerce

Reiman Botanical Gardens

Iowa State University
1407 University Blvd., Ames
515-294-2710
www.reimangardens.com
Open 9–4:30 daily
Admission: $8 adults, $7 seniors, $4 children

Across the street from the veterinary campus and directly south of Jack Trice Stadium, Reiman Gardens has a spectacular butterfly conservatory in addition to the gardens. As might be expected, sustainable practices abound here, and the rose gardens were the first in the country to feature a sustainable design. Rain gardens provide beauty while showcasing smart garden ideas, reduced mowing results in lush lawns, and nursery pots are recycled and reused. Browse for local, organic, and fair trade products in the gift shop.

Boone & Scenic Valley Railroad and Museum

225 10th St., Boone
800-626-0319
www.scenic-valleyrr.com

Take an old-fashioned steam engine train ride over a terrifying wooden suspension bridge on Boone & Scenic Valley line, 20 minutes west of Ames. It offers a wonderful fall foliage tour. Schedules and pricing vary seasonally, with options including a dinner train for $55 and a steam or diesel ride for $25. Children are typically half price.

Des Moines River (1925), *Grant Wood*

28¼ x 24½ n., oil on canvas. Des Moines Art Center Permanent Collections;
Permanent Collections; Bequest of Martha Dunn Trump in memory of
LeRoy C. Dunn, 2002.31. Photo: Ray Andrews

5 DES MOINES
Midwestern Ambitions and Legacy

> *I have been accused of being a flag-waver for my own part*
> *of the country. I do believe in the Middle West—in its peo-*
> *ple and its in its art, and in the future of both.*
>
> —GRANT WOOD,
> *REVOLT AGAINST THE CITY*

This section explores ambition as a theme in Grant Wood's life and work, and how this relates to the state's history and to the art world in general. Wood was clearly as ambitious as he was resilient, as evidenced by his midnight train ride to Minneapolis the same day he graduated from high school, his forays to Europe, and his associations with academic and governmental powers to create leadership roles for himself.

The journey through Des Moines starts at the birthplace of the only U.S. president born in Iowa, Herbert Hoover, and visits the state's capitol building and the governor's mansion, the latter two repositories of Midwestern art. The trek ends at the Des Moines Art Center, where Wood's painting of Herbert Hoover's birthplace can be seen alongside the work of such world-famous artists as Paul Gauguin and Francis Bacon, as well as great American artists Edward Hopper and Jasper Johns. This context encourages an understanding of Wood and his placement in Iowa, in America, and in the world, and it is this

The Des Moines skyline Iowa Tourism Office

Thompson Home in Union Park *(n.d.), Grant Wood*
30 x 36 in., oil on canvas. Des Moines Art Center Permanent
Collections; Bequest of Martha Dunn Trump in memory of
LeRoy C. Dunn, 2002.29. Photo: Ray Andrews

context that reveals the issues dominating provincial art communities around the globe.

Unlike Herbert Hoover, Wood chose art as the vehicle for his political ambitions. It certainly seems to have been a necessary career choice for a man with eccentric and unconventional tastes, and a personal life that remains to this day submerged in speculation. Wood painted several works that address political sentiments and national identity directly, and these paintings remain unique in American history as supreme commentaries on national figures and democratic ideals. His paintings may arguably have had more influence shaping political sensibilities in America in the long run than anything that resulted from Hoover's presidency.

Wood's contact with Des Moines, Iowa's vibrant and expansive capital, seems to have been rather minimal considering his important role as the state's chief artistic mascot. It is interesting to note that Wood chose to maintain his home in Cedar Rapids, though he could have presumably relocated to the capital as his fame increased. However, the legacy of Wood's rambling interests and his massive range of experimentation is readily evident in the contemporary art world of Des Moines. The John and Mary Pappajohn Sculpture Park (see the "Today's Landscape" section in this chapter) is filled with public art manifesting the zeitgeist of Wood and others like him.

As an art center, Des Moines illustrates some of the rather ambiguous reactions to the regional art that Wood typifies. The astounding and not to be missed Des Moines Art Center and, even more so, the Pappajohn Sculpture Park suggest a state connoisseurship intent on showcasing nationally and internationally known art and artists, contributing to the edification of local culture. This makes Des Moines an exciting top stop on the pilgrimage of all discerning art buffs and a good place to see world-renowned art alongside local art. In Des Moines there is little sense of the domination Wood had in the way he is celebrated in the Cedar Rapids Art Museum. Rather, it is a place of more divergent voices, though the scope of John Pappajohn's architectural developments and sculpture park express the mastery and power of a proud art collector and a mover and shaker in the urban environment in quite a substantial way.

The city itself is filled with some important 19th-century buildings, including the capitol building, and like Cedar Rapids and Davenport, it is graced with a long stretch of river with adjacent parks, riverside amphitheaters, walking paths, a pagoda garden, and a botanical center. There's more to see and do than you can pack into one visit, including shopping, sports, and cultural festivals such as the nationally recognized Des Moines Arts Festival (see "Today's Landscape"), which is staged outside on a series of bridges that span the Des Moines River. Des Moines retains its charm and history while offering the amenities of a large city.

Surrounding Des Moines, towns such as Prairie City provide a glance into the historic wildlife of the state. These are the last echoes of a rural Iowa free from industrial, corporately controlled farming and the onslaught of genetically modified agrarian policies that are overrunning the provincial and homespun honesty of Grant Wood's Iowa.

For more information about the area, contact the Greater Des Moines Convention and Visitors Bureau, 400 Locust Street, Suite 265, Des Moines; 515-286-4960 or 800-451-2625; www.desmoinescvb.com.

 BIRTHPLACE OF HERBERT HOOVER

110 Parkside Dr., West Branch
319-643 2541
www.nps.gov/heho

Open 9–5 daily, except major holidays
Admission: museum and library
$6 adults, $3 seniors, and free for children

The birthplace of Herbert Hoover in West Branch is well worth a stop, as a national park–managed attraction in its own right as well as the inspiration for one of Grant Wood's most important paintings, *The Birthplace of Herbert Hoover*. (See "Des Moines Art Center" on page 87 for more information about the painting.) It is adjacent to the Hoover Presidential Library and Museum. West Branch, only a few miles from I-80 and a good pit stop after you leave the Cedar Rapids / Iowa City corridor and head west toward Des Moines or Ames, is a quaint village with authentic "farmer café" cuisine and a historic Victorian-era brick facade Main Street with excellent window shopping.

Like Grant Wood, Herbert Hoover was born in Iowa to devoutly Christian and civil-minded parents. A contemporary of Wood, Hoover, born in 1874, was initially admired nationally for his role directing relief supplies to struggling Europeans after World War I, a role that would eventually help win him the presidency. Hoover was in Europe at approximately the same time that Grant Wood was in France, so the two Iowans shared the formative experience of working in postwar Europe after serving in the military. Hoover went on to become secretary of commerce for presidents Coolidge and Harding before

serving as president himself from 1929 to 1933. Unfortunately, the stock market crash of 1929 and the Great Depression occurred on Hoover's watch, and the nation vilified him for the economic disaster and the lack of efficacy in rectifying the situation when unemployment rose to 25 percent. The fact that Hoover ordered General MacArthur to use tear gas on 15,000 veterans protesting the underpayments of pensions in 1932 didn't help either. Iowans are willing to contextualize Hoover's presidency within a longer career and retain him as a hero still, as he has been the only Iowan elected U.S. president.

Herbert Hoover's birthplace cottage is on the grounds of the presidential library and museum in West Branch   Iowa Tourism Office

 ## PRAIRIE BUFFALO SANCTUARY

Neal Smith National Wildlife Refuge and Prairie Learning and Visitor Center
9981 Pacific St., Prairie City
515-994-3400
www.tallgrass.org

Trails open sunrise–sunset daily; learning center open 9–4 Mon.–Sat. and noon–5 Sun.
Admission: free for visitors center and self-guided car tour

As you head west on I-80, you pass Prairie City, where a pleasant hour can be spent on a car safari through tall grass prairie and free-roaming buffalo and antelope. The several-acre national park allows an uninterrupted view of the horizon and the strong horizontals that Midwesterner Frank Lloyd Wright emphasized in his prairie-style architecture.

The profound tie Wood had with the prairie can be experienced firsthand here. The refuge is a good place to learn more about Iowa's rich prairie heritage, offering elk and buffalo, native flowers and grasses, the auto tour and hiking trails, and a visitors center with state-of-the-art audiovisuals and exhibits dealing with wildlife. Wood was known to be a wildlife enthusiast, and one of his many animal inspirations was the buffalo.

The expanse of the prairie and sky above it makes one consider the relative diminutive size and importance humans hold in the universe and history. The tall grasses and moist soil can swallow up a homestead or field plot in a few short years, erasing all signs of human endeavor. Perhaps Grant Wood felt goaded, rather than intimidated, by the scale and power of these sparse prairie surrounds, and set out to make a bigger and more permanent mark than Iowa farmers could hope to carve for themselves with a plow.

Other attractions in Prairie City include four beautiful parks, the Prairie City Historical Society Museum, a farmer's market held on Thursday in the summer, and dining at places such as Sisters of the Heart Tearoom or Goldie's Restaurant and Ice Cream Shoppe. The annual

See buffalo on the range at Neal Smith Wildlife Refuge and Prairie Learning Center in Prairie City   Iowa Tourism Office

Prairie Days celebration is held in late June. For more information, call the Prairie City City Hall at 515-994-2649.

GOVERNOR'S MANSION

Terrace Hill
2300 Grand Ave.,
Des Moines
515-281-7205 or
515-281-3614

www.terracehilliowa.org
Guided tours at 10:30, 11:30,
12:30, and 1:30; walk-ins welcome
Admission: $5 adults, $2 children

Terrace Hill, a National Historic Landmark, is one of the finest examples of Second Empire Victorian architecture. B. F. Allen, Iowa's first millionaire, built Terrace Hill in 1869; the Hubbell family purchased it in 1884 and donated it to the state in 1971. It has served as the Iowa governor's residence since 1976.

Terrace Hill is open for tours, and the guides are friendly, telling humorous anecdotes of the place. Despite the security at the visitor's entrance, where one is screened for

An interior room of Terrace Hill
Iowa Tourism Office

weapons, the place maintains an intimate and charming period feel. The governor may also appear at any moment from his private quarters. His family does actually live in the building, on the third floor in what were the servants' quarters.

An impressionist landscape painting by Grant Wood is on display on the second floor, which you'll see on the tour. The painting's brush work pays homage to French impressionist painters and documents Grant's initial yearning for European recognition: Although he sought international acclaim for his artwork in France, he failed to have a successful exhibition there. While humble in size, the painting's placement in the governor's mansion is a testament to Wood's success within his own state. A homeboy glorified!

Terrace Hill, the home of the governor, is a national Historic Landmark built in 1869 and houses a Grant Wood painting   Iowa Tourism Office

 ## IOWA STATE CAPITOL

Grand Ave. and E. Ninth,
Des Moines
515-281-5591
www.legis.state.ia.us/Pubinfo/Tour/

Open 8–4:30 Mon.–Fri., 9–4
Sat.; tours every hour, starting
at 9:30 and ending at 2:30
Admission: free

The only state capitol building in the United States with five domes is well worth visiting. Built in 1886 around the time of Wood's birth, it was designed by French architect Alfred Piquenard and Chicago architect John Cochrane. Piquenard originally came to Iowa to join a utopian community in Corning, the home of an Icarian society whose experiments with egalitarianism greatly influenced the thinking of Karl Marx. The French Icarians' utopia only lasted a season.

The century-old building features a 275-foot gold-leafed dome flanked by four smaller domes, a grand staircase, and beautiful woodwork. Atop a hill, it is visible from a long distance, a fantastic and magical presence. Tours, which last 60 minutes, feature the legislative and old supreme court chambers, the governor's office, and the five-story gilded law library with deal-making nooks,

Soldiers and Sailors Monument (1925), *Grant Wood. The state capitol building can be seen in the distance.* 33 x34 in., 1925, oil on canvas. Des Moines Art Center Permanent Collections; Bequest of Martha Dunn Trump in memory of LeRoy C. Dunn, 2002.28. Photo: Ray Andrews

a scale model of the Battleship Iowa, and a collection of first-lady dolls. The grounds include a World War II memorial with a sculpture and Wall of Memories. Other memorials include the 1894 Soldiers and Sailors Monument, honoring the men who fought in the Civil War, and those honoring soldiers who served in the Spanish-American, Korean, and Vietnam wars.

 ## DES MOINES ART CENTER

4700 Grand Ave., Des Moines   *Open 11–4 Tues., Wed., and Fri.;*
515-277-4405   *11–9 Thurs.; 10–4 Sat.; noon–4 Sun.*
www.desmoinesartcenter.org   *Admission: free*

A succinct cultural oasis, this museum is a must-see for art enthusiasts and is an example of modern architecture virtually unrivaled in the entire country. It displays one of Grant Wood's most significant works, *The Birthplace of Herbert Hoover* (see "Birthplace of Herbert Hoover" on page 83 for information about the site), alongside a rich and variegated assortment of 19th-

The Richard Meier–designed wing of the Des Moines Art Center is the newest part of the complex Des Moines Art Center

and 20th-century art. The museum has hosted some very significant contemporary shows, making it exceptionally important at a curatorial level.

The museum offers a celebrated collection of artwork from the 19th century to the present, including artists such as Francis Bacon, Andy Warhol, Anselm Kiefer, and Pablo Picasso; traveling exhibitions; educational and fine arts programs; a museum shop and restaurant; and grounds containing important and noteworthy sculptures. There is also a very fine printing and graphics department that usually hosts an exhibition, drawing upon the substantial collections owned by the museum. The ambitious architectural design of the building and the breadth of its collection demonstrate that the patrons of the art center intended it to be on par with other world-class museums.

An interior view of the I. M. Pei wing, Des Moines Art Center
Des Moines Art Center

Designed in three parts by three world-renowned architects, the museum building represents three distinct decades of American architectural history. One can trace the changes and evolution of style starting with the original museum, designed by Eliel Saarinen, and then proceeding to the "brutalist" sculpture wing, created by I. M. Pei, who also designed the National Museum in Washington and the glass pyramid for the Louvre in Paris. Finally, the newest part of the complex, a striking affair all in white apart from the sumptuously polished wood floors, was designed by the great Richard Meier, famously known as a member of the New York Five and creator of the new Getty in Los Angeles. Do not miss the beautiful huge elevator that doubles as a service lift. It is the size of a sitting room and could quite easily accommodate a dining table, a sofa, and a piano!

Though Wood is interred in Anamosa, perhaps the Des Moines Art Center is symbolically a more fitting place to pay one's respects to the artist and end the Grant Wood–Iowa tour. It's certainly a better place to bid farewell than a cemetery beneath the shadows of a state penitentiary (see part 1). It is here that the results of his ambition can be assessed, he can be seen in the context of world art, and he can be compared with some formidable rivals on the national and international stage. His memory is celebrated in the company of his illustrious peers; his paintings hang alongside works by Edward Hopper and Jean-Baptiste-Camille Corot. Because of its intimate scale and lack of crowds, the museum is an ideal place to contemplate and reflect without any distractions.

The following works at the museum are must-sees.

The Birthplace of Herbert Hoover (1931), Grant Wood

This painting, considered one of the most important of Grant Wood's works, is usually on display. It is but one of several Grant Wood paintings and prints in the museum's collection. (These are not generally displayed, but it may be possible to view them if you make advance arrangements with the curators.) Painted in 1931, it depicts the humble birthplace of a great American president. (For more information about the home, located in West Branch, see "Birthplace of Herbert Hoover" on page 83.) It was painted during the president's third year in office and must have been in part a glorification of the president and his humble Iowa origins.

The painting and its relationship to other works by Wood with political themes further enlarge the vision of a painter working in the tradition of political and patriotic painting, albeit with a sense of irony and humor. Wood's interest in politics and history suggest that he had a strong political agenda and aspirations, perhaps inherited from the socialist tendencies of the Arts and Crafts movement, and that his ambitions were like that of many Americans: without bounds or limits. Wood could create art in many spheres, not just easel painting.

One wonders if Wood didn't consciously choose patriotic themes—such as George Washington cutting down the cherry tree, the midnight ride of Paul Revere, and the birthplace of Herbert Hoover—to win the approval of a larger group of citizens who would be uncritical of the work out of respect for the subject matter. Or was his aim an implied critique and subtle irony? This tradition of American patriotic painting, political and sometimes satirical, remains a deep and absorbing aspect of pictorial production in the

States. Wood's humorous, slightly deprecating, and ironic tone can be compared to artist Jasper Johns, who also depicted patriotic images, in his case American flags imbued with a sense of visual puzzlement. Wood's and Johns's works share a similar unease while at the same time call upon patriotic sensibilities.

The issue of a specific demand for an American painting is one that continues to riddle American artists—whether it be Jackson Pollack, Grant Wood, or Jasper Johns—and Wood attempts to address it in this work. In visual terms it outlines a particular political sensibility, one of belief contrasted with irony: Small-town values, naive stylization, distortions, and parody are deliberately employed to put forth a political position that is not altogether supportive—Hoover was not, in fact, an ideal president. In its most positive interpretation, the painting transcends politics and recalls the precision and refinement of Indian miniatures, celebrating the wealth of color bequeathed by the late angle of the sun on the land and the homespun majesty of a well-known Iowan landscape.

Ville d'Avray: L'Étang et la Maison Cabassud (ca. 1855–1860), Jean-Baptiste-Camille Corot

Celebrated French painter Camille Corot is considered by many to be the father of modern landscape painting—his students gave him the nickname Papa Corot—and this painting is relevant to Grant Wood in many ways. Both Corot and Wood had provincial backgrounds and celebrated the world of the countryside. They were both devoted to nature and had fiercely independent spirits. Corot, more than any other French painter, was responsible for the creation of a school of landscape painting that could claim the likes of Monet, Cézanne, and Pissarro as its descendants. Wood, too, can be seen as an American offspring of this family tree, in his persistent travels to Paris to absorb the lessons of the French school of painting and in his forays into impressionist landscape painting.

Corot and Wood seem to share similar instincts: the desire to render and represent a place dear to the heart, and to give expression to the feelings of connectedness and love one can harbor for one's home. This is evident in Wood's early work, which included several paintings of his grandmother's house and various places he lived during his short, highly energetic life. These early paintings pay homage to the tradition initiated by Corot, which was firmly based on direct observation of nature and works created out-of-doors. Corot never lost the sense of spontaneity and directness that resulted from his response to nature, and this painting, the result of humble ambition, sought more to evoke the lyrical and poetic.

Over time, Wood seems to have abandoned his roots as a painter of direct and spontaneous responses to nature, and in its place he embraced a far more exacting form of painting. In a sense he discarded the gentle poetics of im-

Ville d'Avray:L'Étang et la Maison Cabassud (Ville d'Avray: Pond and Cabassud House, 1855–1860), *Jean-Baptiste-Camille Corot*   18¼ x 21¾ in., oil on canvas. Purchased with funds from the Coffin Fine Arts Trust; Nathan Emory Coffin Collection of the Des Moines Art Center, 1962.20. Photo Rich Sanders

pressionism for a style of painting much more concerned with ambition—and worldly ambition at that. His artistic commentaries on history and politics— as the portrait of Hoover's birthplace indicates—almost suggest that he had ambitions for his political opinions to be taken seriously. The gentle ambition of Corot, which was almost nostalgic in its revelries for past experiences and places but always constant to Corot's inner feelings, was replaced in Wood's work with a hard-hitting and almost brutal rigor in which everything is delineated and no room is left for poetic interpretation. There is still the question as to whether Wood in fact squandered his youthful poetic talent with works that became overly realistic, literal, and propagandistic.

Automat (1927), Edward Hopper

This painting appears as a direct contrast to Grant Wood's work. A depiction of a young woman sitting alone in a diner, it suggests a variety of possible narratives of alienation: The figure is so distraught that she drinks her coffee wearing only one glove. The stairs lead down. When she can prevaricate no longer, she will have to venture out into a threatening gloom. Compared to

Automat *(1927)*, **Edward Hopper** 28 x 36 in., 1927, oil on canvas. Des Moines Art Center Permanent Collections; Purchased with funds from the Edmundson Art Foundation, Inc. 1958.2. Photo: Rich Sanders

Wood's kind of painting, there is a very different and perhaps more modern sensibility at work.

Edward Hopper, Wood's artistic senior, shared similarities with Wood: Both spent time abroad in Paris, absorbing the lessons of the French school and impressionism, and both ultimately returned to the States to find personal styles of their own and become significant painters in their own right. Hopper's career, however, was much more cosmopolitan, and hence he did not have such a negative and provincial bias charged against him. A New York artist and a fairly acclaimed one, his career was longer and more self-assured. Urban scenes dominate his output, and he remained a figurative artist like Wood despite the shift to abstraction in art circles.

Wood had criticized the East Coast and European art establishments and their domination over the art of the Midwest. In his essay *Revolt Against the City,* he asserted, "our Eastern states are still colonies of Europe," and "the long domination of our own art by Europe, and especially by the French, was a deliberately cultivated commercial activity—a business—and dealers connected with the larger New York galleries played into the hands of the French promoters because they themselves found such a connection profitable." Many times Wood ranted against the domination of the East Coast establishment and readily saw a conspiratorial relationship in the world of business and art: "The present revolt against the domination exercised over art and letters and over much of our thinking and living by Eastern capitals of finance and politics brings up many considerations that ought to be widely discussed."

Hopper was an easel painter who never exhibited a predilection for massive social transformation in the way Wood did. Wood's articulated vision of social egalitarianism largely stemmed from his training and participation in the Arts and Crafts movement, with its socialist philosophies.

TODAY'S LANDSCAPE
Ancillary Art and
Ecoattractions

The John and Mary Pappajohn Sculpture Park
13th St. and Grand Ave., Des Moines
515-277-4405
www.desmoinesartcenter.org
Open sunrise–midnight daily
Admission: free

Opened in 2009, this is one of the most significant sculpture parks in the nation, comprising a $40 million collection of more than 25 sculptures, including works by internationally collected sculptors such as Willem de Kooning, Tony Cragg,

Deborah Butterfield, "Ancient Forest" 110 x 144 x 42 in., 2009, bronze   Des Moines Art Center

Debora Butterfield, Barry Flanagan, Sol Lewitt, Jaume Plensa, and others. Sited on 4 acres in the downtown area called the Des Moines Western Gateway, the sculpture park is a collaboration between the Pappajohn family, the City of Des Moines, and the Des Moines Art Center. Guided tours can be requested at the center, and there is also a cell phone tour reached by dialing 515-657-8264. (The phone tour is free, but you have to pay for the minutes.)

A businessman from Iowa, John Pappajohn has sought to earn international recognition in the art world with his private collection and patronage of the arts in the public sector. Similar to the effect Frank Gehry's Guggenheim Museum had on the city of Bilbao in Spain, the sculpture park and urban redevelopment of this area of downtown Des Moines may have been initiated in order to heighten the reputation of Iowa and strengthen business concerns. However, it represents a continuation of Grant Wood's efforts to provide a place for art at the local public level.

The sculpture park is a nice place for a walk.
Iowa Tourism Office

Jaume Plensa, "Nomade" 27 x 17 feet, 2007, painted stainless steel
Des Moines Art Center

Wood's predilection for experimentation, in part deriving from his early interest in the Arts and Crafts movement, encouraged him to work in different mediums, and this is echoed here in the wide assortment of sculptures. Pieces such as Wood's *Lilies of the Alley* (see the "Cedar Rapids Museum of Art" section in chapter 2) could quite easily find a place here if reproduced into a larger sculpture and planted within the aesthetic hodgepodge of this flamboyant and rolling sprawl.

Des Moines Arts Festival
Western Gateway Park, downtown Des Moines
www.desmoinesartsfestival.org
Admission: free

Each year the state's capital hosts the ambitious, nationally recognized Des Moines Arts Festival, which is held in the summer outside on a series of bridges that span the Des Moines River and abuts a riverside amphitheater, walking paths, and a pagoda garden and sculpture garden. This same area is closed to vehicles to become the Downtown Des Moines Farmers' Market on the weekends much of the year. For more information about the festival, including dates (which vary from year to year), consult the festival website or get in touch with the Downtown Community Alliance (515-286-4950; www.downtowndesmoines.com).

Downtown Des Moines Farmers' Market

Court Ave., Des Moines
515-286-4928
www.desmoinesfarmersmarket.com
Open Sat. 7 AM–noon, May 1–Oct. 30

Representing farmers and other purveyors from 51 counties across Iowa, the Downtown Des Moines Farmers' Market presents a delectable assortment of fresh fruit, vegetables, herbs, and flowers, along with local wine, goat cheese, and extraordinary baked goods. The smells are intoxicating. Iowa-raised meat on offer includes buffalo, ostrich, and tilapia.

Jasper Winery

2400 George Flagg Pkwy., Des Moines
515-282-9643
www.jasperwinery.com
Open 10–6 Mon.–Sat. and 1–5 Sun.

Jasper Winery sources its grapes from central Iowa and is conveniently located just two blocks to the west of Grays Lake, on the south side of Waterworks Park, a fine walk in downtown Des Moines.

FARTHER AFIELD

Pottawattamie County Courthouse

227 S. Sixth St., Council Bluffs
712-328-5644 or 712-328-5777
Open 8–4:30 Mon.–Fri.
Admission: free

The restored Grant Wood corn murals from the Chieftain Hotel are displayed in the lobby of the county courthouse. Wood's idea was to make the viewer feel as if he were sitting in the midst of corn stalks, rolling hills, and farms up to the horizon. To a certain extent they recall the great water lilies painted by Monet.

Sioux City Art Center

225 Nebraska St., Sioux City
712-279-6272
www.siouxcityartcenter.org
Open 10–4 Tues., Wed., Fri., and Sat.; 10–9 Thurs.; 1–4 Sun.
Admission: free

This lavish center hosts a museum with exhibition space and education and events spaces. More than a thousand works of art from local national and international artists belong to the museum. There is a collection of Regionalist paintings, and the museum has a very interesting display of Grant Wood's mural work entitled *The Corn Room*. This mural was one of four commissioned by Eugene Eppley for his hotels in Council Bluffs, Cedar Rapids, Waterloo, and Sioux City. *The Corn Room* was created in 1927; it was rediscovered in 1979 under layers of paint and wallpaper, and restored.

Joslyn Art Museum
2200 Dodge St., Omaha, Nebraska
402-342-3300
www.joslyn.org
Open 10–4 Tues.–Wed. and Fri.–Sat., 10–8 Thurs., noon–4 Sun.
Admission: $8 adults, $6 seniors and students, $5 ages 5–17

If you have time to venture farther afield, make a two-hour trip west from Des Moines, crossing the Missouri River on the western frontier of Iowa to reach Nebraska. The Joslyn Museum boasts a strong collection of American art, including *Young Corn,* painted by Wood in the Amana countryside (see part 3).

Loess Hills
Hitchcock Nature Center
27792 Ski Hill Loop, Honey Creek
712-545-3283
Open 6 AM–10 PM daily
Admission: $2 per day or $10 annually

An ecological curiosity to visit en route to Nebraska is the Loess Hills. An extremely rare geological phenomenon, the hills are actually formed by the wind blowing dust and topsoil over the course of a millennium, akin to sand dunes. The only other place in the world with such formations is a small area of China. The hills are thus very fragile and vulnerable to erosion once the prairie grass is plowed, and soil conservation is a concern in this region. Other green initiatives are under way here, including the Loess Hills Lodge at Hitchcock Nature Center, where green building practices are on exhibit, including porous pavement made of recycled demolition materials, water-saving fixtures, energy-efficient products and lighting, and low VOC (volatile organic compounds) materials throughout. Hitchcock Nature Center is located just 20 minutes from downtown Omaha. To get there, follow I-29 to exit 61A. Turn north on the Old Lincoln Highway and follow it 5 miles to Page Lane. Follow signs to the park entrance.

THE FUTURE OF
GRANT WOOD'S IOWA

Modern Transformations in Art and Land Stewardship
in the Twenty-First Century

s the murals of Iowa State University library suggest, the discourse on the role of science in agriculture and home economics was important in Wood's time and remains topical today. As you drive across Iowa, you will be impressed by the large-scale farms and monster equipment that tend them. Monocultures of pesticide-resistant soybean and corn grown using industrial methods on thousand-acre plots cultivated by mammoth machinery worth half a million dollars are a stark visual contrast to the horse farming and manual-labor farm scenes that Wood saw as a boy and represented in his paintings.

Iowa Farm Landscape *(n.d.)*, *Grant Wood*   George T. Henry College Archives, Stewart Memorial Library, Coe College

Prior to World War II, the average farm was smaller than 160 acres, and Iowa was one of the largest grape-producing states in the nation. Grape production all but disappeared, however, when chemical warfare technology was transformed into agricultural chemicals and marketed to farmers. Poisonous chemical drift from neighboring aerial spraying of corn and soybean row crops quickly annihilated fruit trees and grape vineyards in Iowa. Diversified family farming has never been disrupted, however; horse-drawn implements are still used in small scale at the Amish farms in the Kalona area, much like the farming methods Wood's father would have practiced.

An increased awareness of the dangers of chemical effects and the property rights of organic farmers have resulted in increased rediversification of crops in Iowa. Organic agronomy and rural sociology programs, along with an Environmental Creative Writing MFA program, have been established at Iowa State University, which work synergistically to create dialogue and alternatives for the state.

This is not the only way agronomy and art have come together in Iowa. In 1979, the Iowa state legislature passed a law, initiated by state senator John Murray, requiring a percentage of all budgets for public buildings be allocated to purchase artwork for public consumption. In 1980, Iowa State University was given administrative authority over the program, and in 1982 the Art on Campus Collection Program resulted from this. Today the program accounts for the largest collection of public art on a college campus in the nation, consisting of about 500 works of art. This type of dedication to public art is the direct legacy of Grant Wood's leadership, and his belief in the importance of local artists and how public art benefits local communities.

MAPS

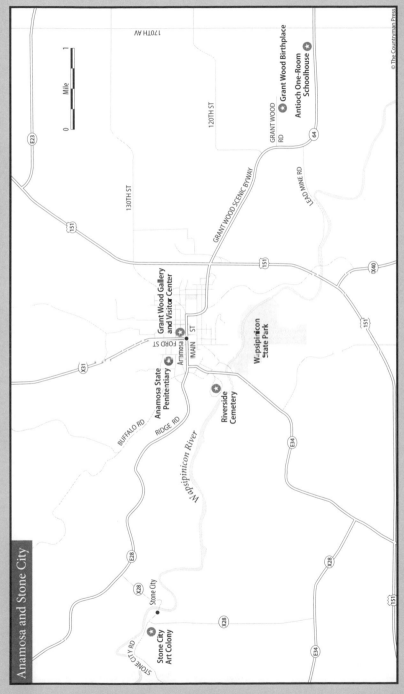

Anamosa and Stone City

170TH AV

120TH ST

Grant Wood Birthplace

Antioch One-Room
Schoolhouse

GRANT WOOD RD

64

LEAD MINE RD

GRANT WOOD SCENIC BYWAY

E23

0   Mile   1

130TH ST

151

151

X40

151

Grant Wood Gallery
and Visitor Center

FORD ST

MAIN ST

Anamosa

Wapsipinicon
State Park

X31

Anamosa State
Penitentiary

BUFFALO RD

RIDGE RD

Riverside
Cemetery

Wapsipinicon River

E34

E28

X28

Stone City

Stone City
Art Colony

STONE CITY RD

X28

X28

E34

151

© The Countryman Press

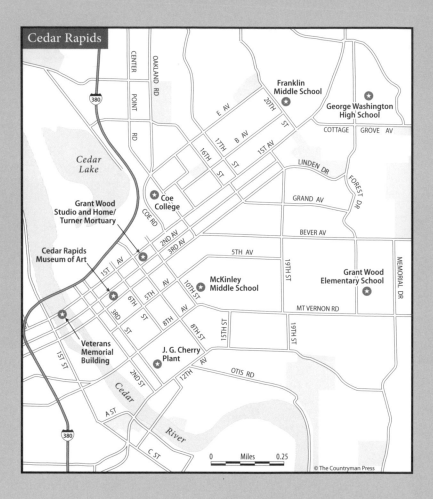

Cedar Rapids

CENTER POINT RD

OAKLAND RD

380

Cedar Lake

E AV

B AV

17TH ST

16TH ST

1ST AV

20TH ST

Franklin Middle School

George Washington High School

COTTAGE   GROVE AV

LINDEN DR

FOREST DR

GRAND AV

Grant Wood Studio and Home/ Turner Mortuary

Coe College

COE RD

2ND AV

3RD AV

5TH AV

BEVER AV

19TH ST

MEMORIAL DR

Cedar Rapids Museum of Art

1ST AV

AV

AV

6TH ST

5TH ST

3RD ST

8TH ST

10TH ST

McKinley Middle School

Grant Wood Elementary School

MT VERNON RD

19TH ST

Veterans Memorial Building

1ST ST

2ND ST

A ST

C ST

8TH ST

12TH ST

15TH ST

J. G. Cherry Plant

8TH AV

OTIS RD

Cedar

River

0   Miles   0.25

© The Countryman Press

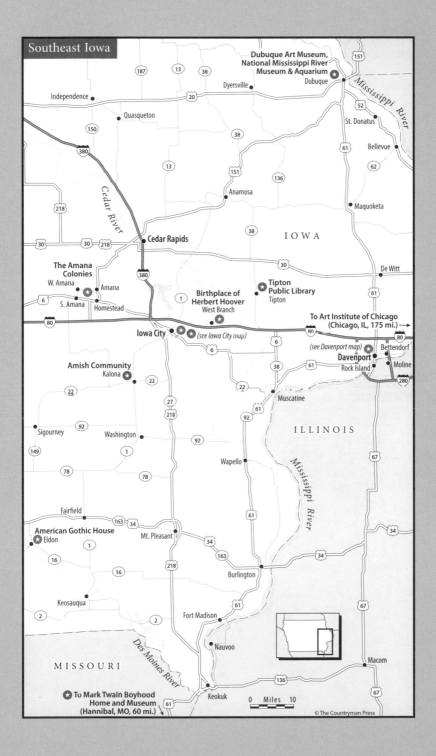

Southeast Iowa

Dubuque Art Museum, National Mississippi River Museum & Aquarium

Dubuque

151

St. Donatus

52

Bellevue

62

Independence

187   13   38

Dyersville

20

Quasqueton

150

380

38

Cedar River

218

13

151   136

Anamosa

Maquoketa

61

IOWA

30

30   218

30

De Witt

61

The Amana Colonies
W. Amana   Amana   380

S. Amana   Homestead

6

1

Birthplace of Herbert Hoover
West Branch

Tipton Public Library
Tipton

38

To Art Institute of Chicago
(Chicago, IL, 175 mi.) →

80   80   6

Iowa City   (see Iowa City map)

6

(see Davenport map)

Bettendorf

Davenport   Moline

Rock Island   280

Amish Community
Kalona   22   22

27

218   38   61

22   22

61

Muscatine

92   92

ILLINOIS

Sigourney   92

Washington   1   92

Wapello

149

78   78

Mississippi River

Fairfield

163   34

American Gothic House
Eldon   1   Mt. Pleasant   34

61   67

16   163

16   218   Burlington   34

34

67

Keosauqua   61

2   2   Fort Madison   67

Nauvoo

MISSOURI

Des Moines River

Macom

136

To Mark Twain Boyhood Home and Museum
(Hannibal, MO, 60 mi.) →   61   Keokuk

0   Miles   10

67

© The Countryman Press

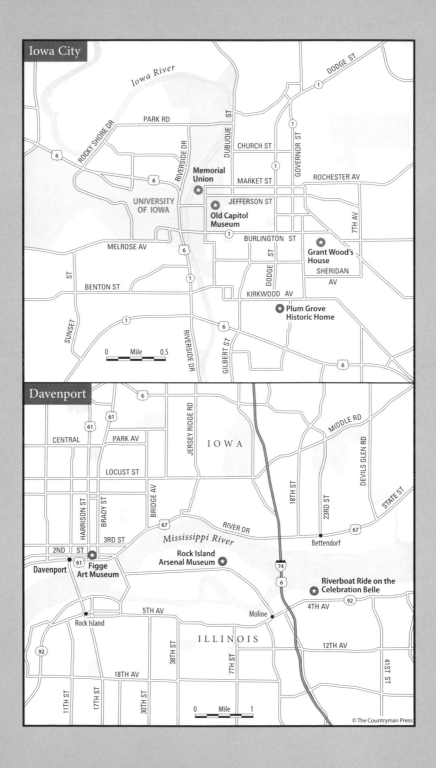

Iowa City

Iowa River

DODGE ST

1

ROCKY SHORE DR

PARK RD

DUBUQUE ST

CHURCH ST

GOVERNOR ST

6

RIVERSIDE DR

1

ROCHESTER AV

Memorial Union

MARKET ST

1

UNIVERSITY OF IOWA

7TH AV

Jefferson St

JEFFERSON ST

Old Capitol Museum

1

BURLINGTON ST

Grant Wood's House

MELROSE AV

6

DODGE ST

SHERIDAN AV

ST

BENTON ST

KIRKWOOD AV

SUNSET

1

RIVERSIDE DR

GILBERT ST

6

Plum Grove Historic Home

6

0   Mile   0.5

Davenport

6

61

61

JERSEY RIDGE RD

MIDDLE RD

CENTRAL

PARK AV

I O W A

DEVILS GLEN RD

LOCUST ST

18TH ST

23RD ST

STATE ST

HARRISON ST

BRADY ST

BRIDGE AV

67

RIVER DR

67

3RD ST

Mississippi River

Bettendorf

2ND ST

61

Figge Art Museum

Davenport

Rock Island Arsenal Museum

74

6

Riverboat Ride on the Celebration Belle

92

5TH AV

Moline

4TH AV

Rock Island

I L L I N O I S

38TH ST

7TH ST

12TH AV

92

41ST ST

11TH ST

17TH ST

30TH ST

18TH AV

0   Mile   1

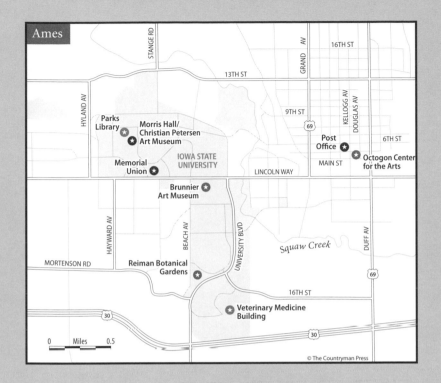

Ames

STANGE RD
GRAND AV
16TH ST
13TH ST
HYLAND AV
9TH ST
KELLOGG AV
DOUGLAS AV
Parks
Library
Morris Hall/
Christian Petersen
Art Museum
6TH ST
Post
Office
Octogon Center
for the Arts
Memorial
Union
IOWA STATE
UNIVERSITY
MAIN ST
LINCOLN WAY
Brunnier
Art Museum
HAYWARD AV
BEACH AV
UNIVERSITY BLVD
Squaw Creek
DUFF AV
MORTENSON RD
Reiman Botanical
Gardens
16TH ST
Veterinary Medicine
Building
0   Miles   0.5
30
30
© The Countryman Press

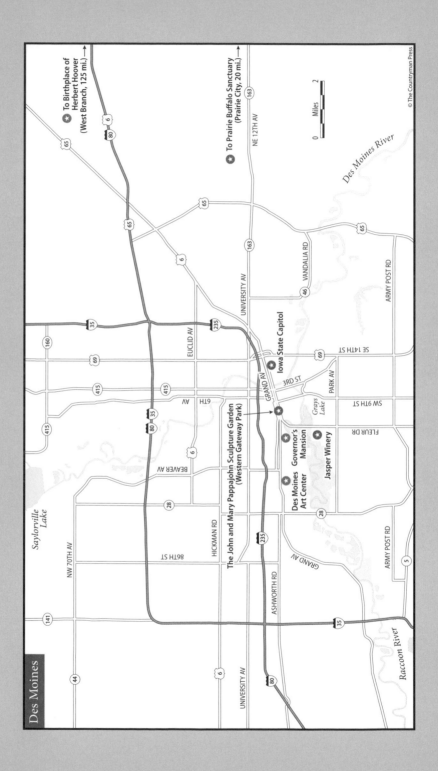

Des Moines

To Birthplace of
Herbert Hoover
(West Branch, 125 mi.)

To Prairie Buffalo Sanctuary
(Prairie City, 20 mi.)

© The Countryman Press

Miles
0   2

Des Moines River

Saylorville
Lake

Grays
Lake

Raccoon River

Iowa State Capitol

Des Moines
Art Center

Governor's
Mansion

Jasper Winery

The John and Mary Pappajohn Sculpture Garden
(Western Gateway Park)

NW 70TH AV

HICKMAN RD

86TH ST

BEAVER AV

6TH AV

EUCLID AV

UNIVERSITY AV

GRAND AV

3RD ST

PARK AV

FLEUR DR

SW 9TH ST

SE 14TH ST

NE 12TH AV

VANDALIA RD

ARMY POST RD

ARMY POST RD

ASHWORTH RD

GRAND AV

UNIVERSITY AV

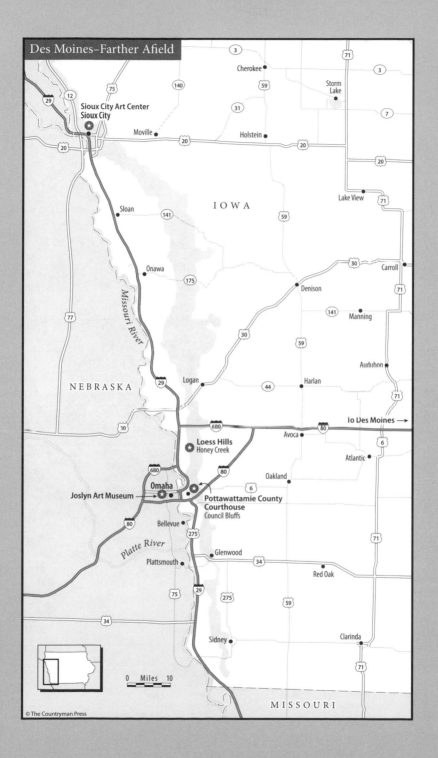

Des Moines–Farther Afield

3

71

Cherokee ●

3

Storm
Lake ●

75

140

59

12

29

75

7

Sioux City Art Center
Sioux City ⭐

31

Moville ●   20   Holstein ●   20

20

20

20

I O W A

Sloan ●   141

59

Lake View ●   71

77

Missouri River

Onawa ●   175

30

Carroll ●

71

Denison ●

141   Manning ●

30

59

Audubon ●

NEBRASKA   29   Logan ●   44   Harlan ●

71

680   80   To Des Moines →

Avoca ●   6

Loess Hills
Honey Creek ⭐   80   Atlantic ●

680   Oakland ●

30   6

Omaha ●   Pottawattamie County
Joslyn Art Museum → ⭐   Courthouse
Council Bluffs ⭐

80   Bellevue ●   275   71

Platte River   Glenwood ●   34

Plattsmouth ●   Red Oak ●

75   29   275   59

34

Clarinda ●

Sidney ●

71

0   Miles   10

MISSOURI

© The Countryman Press

Yellow Doorway, St. Emilion (Porte des Cloitres de l'Eglise Collegiate), *1924, Grant Wood*
Oil on composition board, 16½ x 13 in. Gift of Harriet Y. and John B. Turner II. 72.12.8. Courtesy of Cedar Rapids Museum of Art

INDEX

Dubuque, 62–63
Dubuque Museum of Art, 62
Dunn Funeral Home Patio (Wood), *xxi*

E
Eco-Arts Fest (Cedar Rapids), 43
Eldon, *American Gothic* House, 51–53, *52*
Ely, Henry, 24
Enola Gay, 18
Eppley, Eugene, 96
events. *See* art festivals

F
Fairfield, 51
Fairfield First Fridays Art Walk, 61
Fairfield Visitors Bureau, 51
farmer's markets: Cedar Rapids Downtown Farmer's Market, 40; Davenport Farmer's Market, 60; Des Moines Downtown Farmer's Market, 95; Des Moines Farmers' Market, 95; Iowa City Farmer's Market, 58
Farmer's Son with Watermelon (Wood), 38, *38*
Federal Art Project (FAP), xiv, 71
Feeding the Chickens (Wood) (Anamosa), *3*
festivals. *See* art festivals
Figge Art Museum (Davenport), 50, 55–58
Five Turner Alley (Cedar Rapids), xxi, *27*, 27–29, *28*
Fountain of the Four Seasons (Petersen), 75–76
Franklin Middle School (Cedar Rapids), 34
Fruits of Iowa (Wood), 35–37, *38, 38*

G
gardens. *See* botanical gardens
Garlic Club, 28
Gentle Doctor, The (Petersen), 74–75
Governor's Mansion (Des Moines), 85–86

Graham, Nan Wood, xviii, 3, 18, 27–28, 46
Grant Wood Art Festival (Anamosa), 2, 15
Grant Wood Elementary (Cedar Rapids), 34
Grant Wood Gallery and Visitor Center (Anamosa), 4
Grant Wood Nature Trail, 40
Grant Wood Scenic Byway, 14, 59–60
Grant Wood Studio and Home (Cedar Rapids), 27–29
Grant Wood's House (Iowa City), 48–49
gravesite, in Anamosa, 6–7
Greater Des Moines Convention and Visitors Bureau, 83
greenmarkets. *See* farmer's markets

H
Hancher Auditorium (Iowa City), 59
Hannibal, Missouri, Mark Twain Boyhood Home and Museum, 63
hiking, xv, 84
Hitchcock Nature Center (Omaha), 96
Home of Grant Wood (Cedar Rapids), 27–29
Hoover, Herbert, 81, 82; Birthplace (West Branch), 83–84
Hopper, Edward, *Automat*, 91–93, *92*
Horsetraders, The (Wood), *xxiv*
Houser, Lowell, 67, 77–78

I
Indian Creek (Wood), 34
Iowa Arts Festival (Iowa City), 58–59
Iowa City, 45–63; ancillary art and ecoattractions, 58–63; map, 102; tourist information, 48; Wood sights of interest, 48–58
Iowa City Farmer's Market, 58
Iowa City Visitor Center, 48
Iowa Farm Landscape (Wood), 97
Iowa State Capitol (Des Moines), 86–87